AMONG THE SIOUX

AMONG THE SIOUX

ROBERT J. CRESWELL,
DAVID R. BREED

ISBN: 978-93-5420-024-3

Published: 1906

LECTOR HOUSE LLP
E-MAIL: lectorpublishing@gmail.com

AMONG THE SIOUX

A STORY OF THE TWIN CITIES AND THE TWO DAKOTAS

BY

THE REV. R. J. CRESWELL

Author of "WHO SLEW ALL THESE," ETC.

**WITH INTRODUCTION BY
THE REV. DAVID R. BREED, D.D.**

1906

OUR PLATFORM.

For Indians we want American Education, American homes,
American rights,—the result of which is American citizenship.
And the Gospel is the power of God for their salvation!

DEDICATION.

TO NELLIE,

(MY WIFE)

Who, for forty years has been my faithful companion in the toils and triumphs of missionary service for the Freedmen of the Old Southwest and the heroic pioneers of the New Northwest, this volume is affectionately inscribed.

By the Author,
R. J. Creswell.

INTRODUCTION
BY THE REV. DAVID R. BREED, D.D.

The sketches which make up this little volume are of absorbing interest, and are prepared by one who is abundantly qualified to do so. Mr. Creswell has had large personal acquaintance with many of those of whom he writes and has for years been a diligent student of missionary effort among the Sioux. His frequent contributions to the periodicals on this subject have received marked attention. Several of them he gathers together and reprints in this volume, so that while it is not a consecutive history of the Sioux missions it furnishes an admirable survey of the labors of the heroic men and women who have spent their lives in this cause, and furnishes even more interesting reading in their biographies that might have been given upon the other plan.

During my own ministry in Minnesota, from 1870 to 1885, I became very intimate with the great leaders of whom Mr. Creswell writes. Some of them were often in my home, and I, in turn, have visited them. I am familiar with many of the scenes described in this book. I have heard from the missionaries' own lips the stories of their hardships, trials and successes. I have listened to their account of the great massacre, while with the tears flowing down their cheeks they told of the desperate cruelty of the savages, their defeat, their conversion, and their subsequent fidelity to the men and the cause they once opposed. I am grateful to Mr. Creswell for putting these facts into permanent shape and bespeak for his volume a cordial reception, a wide circulation, and above all, the abundant blessing of God.

DAVID R. BREED.

Allegheny, Pa., January, 1906.

PREFACE.

This volume is not sent forth as a full history of the Sioux Missions. That volume has not yet been written, and probably never will be.

The pioneer missionaries were too busily engaged in the formation of the Dakota Dictionary and Grammar, in the translation of the Bible into that wild, barbaric tongue; in the preparation of hymn books and text books:—in the creation of a literature for the Sioux Nation, to spend time in ordinary literary work. The present missionaries are overwhelmed with the great work of ingathering and upbuilding that has come to them so rapidly all over the widely extended Dakota plains. These Sioux missionaries were and are men of deeds rather than of words,—more intent on the *making* of history than the *recording* of it. They are the noblest body of men and women that ever yet went forth to do service, for our Great King, on American soil.

For twenty years it has been the writer's privilege to mingle intimately with these missionaries and with the Christian Sioux; to sit with them at their great council fires; to talk with them in their teepees; to visit them in their homes; to meet with them in their Church Courts; to inspect their schools; to worship with them in their churches; and to gather with them on the greensward under the matchless Dakota sky and celebrate together with them the sweet, sacramental service of our Lord and Savior, Jesus the Christ.

He was so filled and impressed by what he there saw and heard, that he felt impelled to impart to others somewhat of the knowledge thus gained; in order that they may be stimulated to a deeper interest in, and devotion to the cause of missions on American soil.

In the compilation of this work the author has drawn freely from these publications, viz.:

THE GOSPEL OF THE DAKOTAS,	
MARY AND I,	*By Stephen R. Riggs, D.D., LL.D.*
TWO VOLUNTEER MISSIONARIES,	*By S. W. Pond, Jr.*
INDIAN BOYHOOD,	*By Charles Eastman*
THE PAST MADE PRESENT,	*By Rev. William Fiske Brown*
THE WORD CARRIER,	*By Editor A. L. Riggs, D.D.*
THE MARTYRS OF WALHALLA,	*By Charlotte O. Van Cleve*
THE LONG AGO,	*By Charles H. Lee*

The Dakota Mission,   *By Dr. L. P. Williamson and others*

Dr. T. S. Williamson,   *By Rev. R. McQuesten*

He makes this general acknowledgment, in lieu of repeated references, which would otherwise be necessary throughout the book. For valuable assistance in its preparation he is very grateful to many missionaries, especially to John P. Williamson, D.D., of Grenwood, South Dakota; A. L. Riggs, D.D. of Santee, Nebraska; Samuel W. Pond, Jr., of Minneapolis, and Mrs. Gideon H. Pond, of Oak Grove, Minnesota. All these were sharers in the stirring scenes recorded in these pages. The names Dakota and Sioux are used as synonyms and the English significance instead of the Indian cognomens.

May the blessing of Him who dwelt in the Burning Bush, rest upon all these toilers on the prairies of the new Northwest.

R. J. Creswell.

Minneapolis, Minnesota, January, 1906.

CONTENTS

PART I.
SOWING AND REAPING.

PART II.
SOME SIOUX STORIETTES.

CONTENTS xi

PART I.
SOWING AND REAPING.

FORT SNELLING.

They that sow in tears shall reap in joy.
He that goeth forth and weepeth, bearing
Precious Seed,
Shall doubtless come again
With rejoicing,
Bringing his sheaves.

Psalm 126.

AMONG THE SIOUX.

CHAPTER I.

The Pond Brothers.—Great Revival.—Conversions.—Galena.—Rum-seller Decision.— Westward.—Fort Snelling.—Man of-the-Sky.—Log Cabin.—Dr. Williamson.—Ripley.— Lane Seminary.—St. Peters Church.—Dr. Riggs.—New England Mary.—Lac-qui-Parle.

Now appear the flow'rets fair
Beautiful beyond compare
And all nature seems to say,
"Welcome, welcome, blooming May."

It was 1834. A lovely day—the opening of the merry month of May!

The Warrior, a Mississippi steamer, glided out of Fever River, at Galena, Illinois, and turned its prow up the Mississippi. Its destination was the mouth of the St. Peters—now Minnesota River—five hundred miles to the north—the port of entry to the then unknown land of the Upper Mississippi.

The passengers formed a motley group; officers, soldiers, fur-traders, adventurers, and two young men from New England. These latter were two brothers, Samuel William and Gideon Hollister Pond, from Washington, Connecticut. At this time, Samuel the elder of the two, was twenty-six years of age and in form, tall and very slender as he continued through life. Gideon, the younger and more robust brother was not quite twenty-four, more than six feet in height, strong and active, a specimen of well developed manhood. With their clear blue eyes, and their tall, fully developed forms, they must have attracted marked attention even among that band of brawny frontiersmen.

In 1831 a gracious revival had occurred in their native village of Washington. It was so marked in its character, and permanent in its results, that it formed an epoch in the history of that region and is still spoken of as "the great revival". For months, during the busiest season of the year, crowded sunrise prayer-meetings were held daily and were well attended by an agricultural population, busily engaged every day in the pressing toil of the harvest and the hayfields. Scores were converted and enrolled themselves as soldiers of the cross.

Among these were the two Pond brothers. This was, in reality with them, the beginning of a new life. From this point in their lives, the inspiring motive, with both these brothers, was a spirit of intense loyalty to their new Master and a burning love for the souls of their fellowmen. Picked by the Holy Spirit out of more than one hundred converts for special service for the Lord Jesus Christ, the Pond brothers resolutely determined to choose a field of very hard service, one to which no others desired to go. In the search for such a field, Samuel the elder brother, journeyed from New Haven to Galena, Illinois, and spent the autumn and winter of 1833-34 in his explorations. He visited Chicago, then a struggling village of a few hundred inhabitants and other embryo towns and cities. He also saw the Winnebago Indians and the Pottawatomies, but he was not led to choose a field of labor amongst any of these.

A strange Providence finally pointed the way to Mr. Pond. In his efforts to reform a rumseller at Galena, he gained much information concerning the Sioux Indians, whose territory the rumseller had traversed on his way from the Red River country from which he had come quite recently. He represented the Sioux Indians as vile, degraded, ignorant, superstitious and wholly given up to evil.

"There," said the rumseller, "is a people for whose souls nobody cares. They are utterly destitute of moral and religious teachings. No efforts have ever been made by Protestants for their salvation. If you fellows are looking, in earnest, for a *hard job*, there is one ready for you to tackle on those bleak prairies."

This man's description of the terrible condition of the Sioux Indians in those times was fairly accurate. Those wild, roving and utterly neglected Indians were proper subjects for Christian effort and promised to furnish the opportunities for self-denying and self-sacrificing labors for which the brothers were seeking.

Mr. Pond at once recognized this peculiar call as from God. After prayerful deliberation, Samuel determined to write to his brother Gideon, inviting the latter to join him early the following spring, and undertake with him an independent mission to the Sioux.

He wrote to Gideon:—"I have finally found the field of service for which we have long been seeking. It lies in the regions round about Fort Snelling. It is among the savage Sioux of those far northern plains. They are an ignorant, savage and degraded people. It is said to be a very cold, dreary, storm-swept region. But we are not seeking a soft spot to rest in or easy service. So come on."

Despite strong, almost bitter opposition from friends and kinsmen, Gideon accepted and began his preparations for life among the Indians, and in March, 1834, he bade farewell to his friends and kindred and began his journey westward.

Early in April, he arrived at Galena, equipped for their strange, Heaven-inspired mission. He found his brother firmly fixed in his resolution to carry out the plans already decided upon. In a few days we find them on the steamer's deck, moving steadily up the mighty father of waters, towards their destination. "This *is* a serious undertaking," remarked the younger brother as they steamed northward. And such it was. There was in it no element of attractiveness from a human view-point.

They expected to go among roving tribes, to have no permanent abiding place and to subsist as those wild and savage tribes subsisted. Their plan was a simple and feasible one, as they proved by experience, but one which required large stores of faith and fortitude every step of the way. They knew, also, that outside of a narrow circle of personal friends, none knew anything of this mission to the Sioux, or felt the slightest interest in its success or failure. But undismayed they pressed on.

The scenery of the Upper Mississippi is still pleasing to those eyes, which behold it, clothed in its springtime robes of beauty. In 1834, this scenery shone forth in all the primeval glory of "nature unmarred by the hand of man."

SAMUEL W. POND,

20 Years a Missionary to the Sioux.

As the steamer Warrior moved steadily on its way up the Mississippi, the rich May verdure, through which they passed, appeared strikingly beautiful to the two brothers, who then beheld it for the first time. It was a most delightful journey and ended on the sixth day of May, at the dock at old Fort Snelling.

This was then our extreme outpost of frontier civilization. It had been established in 1819, as our front-guard against the British and Indians of the Northwest. It was located on the high plateau, lying between the Mississippi and the Minnesota (St. Peters) rivers, and it was then the only important place within the limits of the present state of Minnesota.

GIDEON H. POND,

For Twenty years Missionary to the Dakotas.

While still on board the Warrior, the brothers received a visit and a warm welcome from the Rev. William T. Boutell, a missionary of the American Board to the Ojibways at Leach Lake, Minnesota. He was greatly rejoiced to meet "these dear brethren, who, from love to Christ and for the poor red man, had come alone to this long-neglected field."

A little later they stepped ashore, found themselves in savage environments and face to face with the grave problems they had come so far to solve. They were men extremely well fitted, mentally and physically, naturally and by training for the toils and privations of the life upon which they had now entered. Sent, not by man but by the Lord; appointed, not by any human authority but by the great Jehovah; without salary or any prospects of worldly emoluments, unknown, unheralded, those humble but heroic men began, in dead earnest, their grand life-work. Their mission and commission was to conquer that savage tribe of fierce, prairie warriors, by the two-edged sword of the spirit of the living God and to mold them aright, by the power of the Gospel of His Son. And God was with them as they took up their weapons (not carnal but spiritual) in this glorious warfare.

They speedily found favor with the military authorities, and with one of the most prominent chieftains of that time and region—Cloudman or Man-of-the-sky.

The former gave them full authority to prosecute their mission among the Indians; the latter cordially invited them to establish their residence at his village on the shore of Lake Calhoun.

The present site of Minneapolis was then simply a vast, wind-swept prairie, uninhabited by white men. A single soldier on guard at the old government sawmill at St. Anthony Falls was the only representative of the Anglo-Saxons, where now dwell hundreds of thousands of white men of various nationalities.

Busy, bustling, beautiful Minneapolis, with its elegant homes; its commodious churches; its great University—with its four thousand students—; its well-equipped schools—with their forty-two thousand pupils—; its great business blocks; its massive mills; its humming factories; its broad avenues; its pleasant parks; its population of a quarter of a million of souls; all this had not then even been as much as dreamed of.

Four miles west of St. Anthony Falls, lies Lake Calhoun, and a short distance to the south is Lake Harriet, (two most beautiful sheets of water, both within the present limits of Minneapolis). The intervening space was covered by a grove of majestic oaks.

Here, in 1834, was an Indian village of five hundred Sioux. Their habitations were teepees, made of tamarack bark or of skins of wild beasts. Their burial ground covered a part of lovely Lakewood, the favorite cemetery of the city of Minneapolis. This band recognized Cloudman or Man-of-the-sky as their chief, whom they both respected and loved. He was then about forty years of age. He was an intelligent man, of an amiable disposition and friendly to the approach of Civilization. Here, under the auspices of this famous chieftain, they erected for themselves a snug, little home, near the junction of Thirty-fifth street and Irving Avenue South, Minneapolis.

It was built of large oak logs. The dimensions were twelve feet by sixteen and eight feet high. Straight tamarack poles formed the timbers of the roof. The roof itself was the bark of trees, fastened with strings of the inner bark of the basswood.

A partition of small logs divided the house into two rooms. The ceiling was of slabs from the old government sawmill at St. Anthony Falls. The door was made of boards, split from a tree with an axe, and had wooden hinges and fastenings and was locked by pulling in the latch-string. The single window was the gift of the kind-hearted Major Taliaferro, the United States Indian agent at Fort Snelling. The cash cost of the whole was one shilling, New York currency, for nails, used about the door. The formal opening was the reading of a portion of Scripture and prayer. The banquet consisted of mussels from the Lake, flour and water. This cabin was the first house erected within the present limits of Minneapolis; it was the home of the first citizen settlers of Minnesota and was the first house used as a school-room and for divine worship in the state. It was a noble testimony to the faith, zeal and courage of its builders. Here these consecrated brothers inaugurated their great work. In 1839 it was torn down for materials with which to construct breastworks for the defense of the Sioux, after the bloody battle of Rum River, against their feudal foes, the Ojibways. Here amid such lovely natural surroundings were the very beginnings of this mighty enterprise.

The first lesson was given early in May, by Samuel Pond to Big Thunder chieftain of the Kaposia band, whose teepees were scattered over the bluffs, where now stands the city of St. Paul. His chief soldier was Big Iron. His son was Little Crow, who became famous or rather infamous, as the leader against the whites in the terrible tragedy of '62. Later in May the second lesson was taught by Gideon Pond to members of the Lake Calhoun band. Both lessons were in the useful and civilizing art of plowing and were the first in that grand series of lessons, covering more than seventy years, and by which the Sioux nation have been lifted from savagery to civilization.

While God was preparing the Pond brothers in the hill country of Connecticut for their peculiar life-work, and opening up the way for them to engage in it, He also had in training in the school of His Providences, in Massachusetts and Ohio, fitting helpers for them in this great enterprise. In the early 30's, at Ripley, Ohio, Dr. Thomas S. Williamson and Mrs. Margaret Poage Williamson, a young husband and wife, were most happily located, in the practice of his profession and in the upbuilding of a happy Christian home. To this young couple the future seemed full of promise and permanent prosperity. Children were born to them; they were prosperous and an honorable name was being secured through the faithful discharge of the duties of his most noble profession and of Christian citizenship. They regarded themselves as happily located for life.

The mission call to Dr. and Mrs. Williamson was emphasized by the messenger of death. When the missionary call first came to them, they excused themselves on account of their children. God removed the seeming obstacles, one by one. The little ones were called to the arms of Jesus. "A great trial!" A great blessing also. The way was thus cleared from a life of luxury and ease in Ohio to one of great denial and self sacrifice on mission fields. The bereaved parents recognized this call as from God, and by faith, both father and mother were enabled to say, "Here are we; send us."

"This decision," says an intimate friend, "neither of them after for one moment regretted; neither did they doubt that they were called of God to this great work, nor did they fear that their life-work would prove a failure." With characteristic devotion and energy, Dr. Williamson put aside a lucrative practice, and at once, entered on a course of preparation for his new work for which his previous life and training had already given him great fitness.

In 1833, he put himself under the care of the Presbytery of Chillicothe, removed with his family to Walnut Hills, Cincinnati, and entered Lane Seminary. While the Pond brothers in their log cabin at Lake Calhoun were studying the Sioux language, Dr. Williamson was completing his theological course on the banks of the beautiful river. He was ordained to the office of the gospel ministry in 1834. And in May, 1835, he landed at Fort Snelling with another band of missionaries. He was accompanied by his quiet, lovely, faithful wife, Margaret, and one child, his wife's sister, Sarah Poage, afterwards Mrs. Gideon H. Pond, Mr. and Mrs. Alexander G. Huggins and two children. Mr. Huggins came as a teacher and farmer. During a stay of a few weeks here, Dr. Williamson presided at the organization of the first Protestant congregation in Minnesota, which was called the Presbyterian church of St. Peters. It consisted of officers, soldiers, fur-traders, and members of the mission families—twenty-one in all; seven of whom were received on confession of faith. It was organized at Fort Snelling, June 11, 1835, and still exists as the First Presbyterian church of Minneapolis, with more than five hundred members.

THE OLD FORT SNELLING CHURCH DEVELOPED.

Early in July, Dr. Williamson pushed on in the face of grave difficulties, two hundred miles to the west, to the shores of Lac-qui-Parle, the Lake-that-speaks. Here they were cordially welcomed by Joseph Renville, that famous Brois Brule trader, the half-breed chief who ruled that region for many years, by force of his superior education and native abilities, and who ever was a strong and faithful friend of the missionaries. He gave them a temporary home and was helpful in many ways. Well did the Lord repay him for his kindness to His servants. His wife became the first full-blood Sioux convert to the Christian faith, and his youngest son, John Baptiste Renville, then a little lad, became the first native Presbyterian minister, one of the acknowledged leaders of his people.

AT LAKE MINNETONKA.

June, 1837, another pair of noble ones joined the ranks of the workers by the Lakeside. These were the Rev. Stephen Return Riggs and his sweet New England Mary, he was a native of the beautiful valley of the Ohio; she was born amid the green hills of Massachusetts. His father was a Presbyterian elder of Steubenville, Ohio; her mother was a daughter of New England. She herself was a pupil of the cultured and sainted Mary Lyon of Mount Holyoke.

They were indeed choice spirits, well-fitted by nature and by training for a place in that heroic band, which God was then gathering together on the shores of Lakes Calhoun and Harriet and Lac-qui-Parle, for the conquest of the fiercest tribe of prairie warriors that ever roamed over the beautiful plains of the New Northwest. He was a scholar and a linguist; courageous, energetic, firm, diplomatic; she was cultured, gentle, tactful, and withal, both were intensely spiritual and deeply devoted to the glorious work of soul-winning. Both had been trained as missionaries, with China as a prospective field of service. Step by step in the Providence of God, they were drawn together as life companions and then turned from the Orient to the Western plains.

During these years of beginnings, Dr. Williamson formed the acquaintance of Stephen R. Riggs, then a young man, which culminated in a life-long alliance of love and service. During his seminary course, Mr. Riggs received a letter from his missionary friend, to which he afterwards referred thus: "It seems to me now, strange that he should have indicated in that letter the possible line of work open to me, which has been so closely followed. I remember especially the prominence he gave to the thought that the Bible should be translated into the language of the Dakotas. Men do sometimes yet write as they were moved by the Holy Ghost. That letter decided my going westward rather than to China." It was a lovely day, the first of June, when this young bride and groom arrived at Fort Snelling. Though it was their honeymoon, they did not linger long in the romantic haunts of Minnehaha and the Lakes; but pressed on to Lac-qui-Parle and joined hands with the toilers there in their mighty work of laying foundations broad and deep in the wilderness, like the coral workers in the ocean depths, out of sight of man.

A PARK DRIVE, LAKE CALHOUN.

What a glorious trio of mission family bands were then gathered on Minnesota's lovely plains, on the shores of those beautiful lakes! Pond, Williamson, Riggs. Names that will never be forgotten while a Sioux Christian exists in earth or glory.

SOLDIERS' HOME.

When the American Mission Hall of Fame shall be erected these three names will shine out high upon the dome like "apples of gold in pictures of silver," Pond,

Williamson, Riggs. "And a book of remembrance was written before him for them that feared the Lord and that thought upon his name. * * * And they shall be mine, saith the Lord of hosts, in that day when I make up my jewels."

CHAPTER II.

In 1836, within one year from the arrival of Dr. Williamson and his missionary party at Lac-qui-Parle, a church was organized, with six native members, which in 1837, consisted of seven Dakotas, besides half-breeds and whites, and, within five years, had enrolled forty-nine native communicants. Of this congregation Alexander G. Huggins and Joseph Renville were the ruling elders.

An adobe church edifice was erected in 1841, which for eighteen years met the wants of this people. In its belfry was hung the first church bell that ever rang out over the prairies of Minnesota, the sweet call to the worship of the Savior of the human race. The services of the church were usually held in the native language. The hymns were sung to French tunes, which were then the most popular. At the beginning, translations from the French of a portion of Scripture were read and some explanatory remarks were made by Joseph Renville.

The first school for teaching Indians to read and write in the Dakota language, was opened in December, 1835, at Lac-qui-Parle, in a conical Dakota tent, twenty feet in height and the same in diameter. At first the men objected to being taught for various frivolous reasons, but they were persuaded to make the effort. The school apparatus was primitive and mainly extemporized on the spot. Progress was slow; the attendance small and irregular, but in the course of three months, they were able to write to each other on birch bark. Those who learned to read and write the language properly, soon became interested in the gospel. The first five men, who were gathered into the church, were pupils of this first school. Of the next twenty, three were pupils and fourteen were the kindred of its pupils. Among their descendants were three Dakota pastors and many of the most faithful and fruitful communicants.

One large log-house of five rooms, within the Renville stockade, furnished a home for the three mission families of Dr. Williamson, Rev. Stephen R. Riggs and Gideon H. Pond. One room was both church and school room for years. Under this roof the missionaries met frequently for conference, study and translation of the word of God. Here, September 30, 1844, the original Dakota Presbytery was organized.

MINNEAPOLIS IN 1857.

For several years most of the members of this congregation were women. Once in the new and then unfinished church edifice, more than one hundred Indian men were gathered. When urged to accept Christ and become members of this church, they replied that the church was made up of squaws. Did the missionaries suppose the braves would follow the lead of squaws? Ugh! Ugh!!

For the first seven years, at Lac-qui-Parle, mission work was prosecuted, with marked success in spite of many grave hindrances. But for the four years following—1842-46—the work was seriously retarded. The crops failed and the savages charged their misfortunes to the missionaries. They became very ugly, and began a series of petty yet bitter persecutions against the Christian Indians and the missionaries. The children were forbidden to attend school; the women who favored the church had their blankets cut to pieces and were shut away from contact with the mission. The cattle and horses of the mission were killed, and for a season the Lord's work was stayed at Lac-qui-Parle. Discouraged, but not dismayed His servants were watchful for other opportunities of helpful service.

In 1846, the site of the present, prosperous city of St. Paul, was occupied by a few shanties, owned by "certain lewd fellows of the baser sort," sellers of rum to the soldiers and the Indians. Nearby, scattered over the bluffs, were the teepees of Little Crow's band, forming the Sioux village of Kaposia. In 1846, Little Crow, their belligerent chieftain, was shot by his own brother, in a drunken revel. He survived the wound, but apparently alarmed at the influence of these modern harpies over himself and his people, he visited Fort Snelling and begged a missionary for his village. The United States agent stationed there forwarded this petition to Lac-qui-Parle with the suggestion that Dr. Williamson be transferred to Kaposia. The invitation was accepted by the doctor, so in November, 1846, he became a resident of Kaposia (now South St. Paul). To this new station, he carried the same energy, hopefulness and devotion, he had shown at the beginning. Here he remained six years, serving not only the Indians of Little Crow's band, but also doing great good to the white settlers, who were then gathering around the future Capital City of Minnesota. Here in 1848, he organized an Indian church of eight members. It increased to fifteen members, in 1851, when the Indians were removed.

Then followed the treaty of 1851, which was of great import, both to the white man and to the red man. By this treaty, the fertile valley of the Minnesota was thrown open for settlement to the whites. This took away from the Sioux their hunting-grounds, their cranberry marshes, their deer-parks and the graves of their ancestors. So the Dakotas of the Mississippi and lower Minnesota packed up their teepees, their household goods and gods, some in canoes, some on ponies, some on dogs, some on the women, and slowly and sadly took up their line of march towards the setting of the sun.

No sooner did the Indians move than Dr. Williamson followed them and established a new station at Yellow Medicine, on the West bank of the Minnesota river and three miles above the mouth of the Yellow Medicine river. The first winter there, was a fight for life. The house was unfinished; a very severe winter set in unusually early, the snows were deep and the drifts terrible; the supply-teams were snowed in; the horses perished, the provisions were abandoned to the wolves and the drivers reached home in a half-frozen condition. But God cared for His servants. In this emergency, the Rev. M. N. Adams, of Lac-qui-Parle, performed a most heroic act. In mid-winter, with the thermometer many degrees below zero, he hauled flour and other provisions for the missionaries, on a hand sled, from Lac-qui-Parle to Yellow Medicine, a distance of thirty-two miles. The fish gathered in shoals, an unusual occurrence, near the mission and both the Indians and the missionaries lived through that terrible winter. Here, an Indian church of seventeen members was organized by Dr. Williamson. It increased to a membership of thirty in the next decade.

In March, 1854, the mission houses at Lac-qui-Parle were destroyed by fire. A consolidation of the mission forces was soon after effected. Dr. Riggs and other helpers were transferred from Lac-qui-Parle to a point two miles distant from Yellow Medicine and called Omehoo (Hazelwood). A comfortable mission home was erected. The native Christians removed from Lac-qui-Parle and re-established their homes at Hazelwood. A boarding school was soon opened at this point by Rev. M. N. Adams. A neat chapel was also erected. A church of thirty members was organized by Mr. Riggs. It grew to a membership of forty-five before the massacre. These were mainly from the the Lac-qui-Parle church which might be called the mother of all the Dakota churches.

There were now gathered around the mission stations, quite a community of young men, who had to a great extent, become civilized. With civilization came new wants—pantaloons and coats and hats. There was power also in oxen and wagons and brick-houses. The white man's axe and plow and hoe had been introduced and the red man was learning to use them. So the external civilization went on.

But the great and prominent force was in the underlying education and especially in the vitalizing and renewing power of Christian truth. So far as the inner life was changed, civilized habits became permanent; otherwise they were shadows. Evangelization was working out civilization. It is doing its permanently blessed work even yet.

About this time occurred the formation of the Hazelwood Republic.

This was a band of Indians somewhat advanced in civilization, who were organized chiefly by the efforts of Dr. Riggs, under a written constitution and by-laws. Their officers were a President, Secretary and three judges, who were elected by a vote of the membership for a term of two years each. Paul Maza-koo-ta-mane was the first president and served for two terms. This was an interesting experiment, in the series of efforts, by the missionaries, to change this tribe of nomads from their roving teepee life to that of permanent dwellers in fixed habitations. The rude shock of savage warfare, which soon after revolutionized the whole Sioux nation, swept it away before its efficiency could be properly tested. Surely it was a novelty—an Indian band, regulated by written laws and governed by officers, elected by themselves for a term of years. It now exists only in the memory of the oldest of the tribesmen or the missionaries.

In 1843, a new station was established at Traverse des Sioux (near St. Peter,

Minnesota,) by the Rev. Stephen R. Riggs. This station was doomed to a tragic history. July 15, 1843, Thomas Longley, the favorite brother of Mrs. Mary Riggs, was suddenly swallowed up in the treacherous waters of the Minnesota and laid to rest under what his sister was wont to call the "Oaks of weeping" — three dwarf oaks on a small knoll. In 1844, Robert Hopkins and his young bride joined the workers here. In 1851, July 4, Mr. Hopkins was suddenly swept away to death by the fatal waves of the Minnesota and his recovered body was laid to rest under the oaks where Thomas Longley had slept all alone for seven years. Thus the mission at Traverse des Sioux was closed by the messenger of death. It was continued, however, in the nearby frontier town of St. Peter, whose white settlers requested the Rev. M. N. Adams, one of the missionaries to the Sioux, to devote his time to their spiritual needs. He complied and founded a white Presbyterian church and it is one of the strong Protestant organizations of Southern Minnesota.

In 1843, also the Pond brothers established a station at Oak Grove, twelve miles west of the Falls of St. Anthony. It was never abandoned. For many years it was the center of beneficent influences to both races for miles around. It developed into the white Presbyterian church of Oak Grove, which still stands as a monument to the many noble qualities of its founder, Rev. Gideon Hollister Pond. On the Sabbath scores of his descendants worship within its walls. The surrounding community is composed largely of Ponds and their kindred.

In 1846, a mission was established at Red Wing by the Reverends J. F. Aiton and J. W. Hancock, and another in 1860, at Red Wood by Rev. John P. Williamson.

In 1858, a church was organized at Red Wing with twelve members. This was swept away by the outbreak in 1862.

Dr. John P. Williamson, who was born in 1835, in one of the mission cabins on the shores of Lac-qui-Parle, who has spent his whole life among the Sioux Indians, and who with a singleness of purpose, worthy of the apostle Paul, has devoted his whole life to their temporal and spiritual uplift, thus vividly sketches missionary life among the Sioux in his boyhood days: "My first serious impression of life was that I was living under a great weight of something, and as I began to discern more clearly, I found this weight to be the all-surrounding overwhelming presence of heathenism, and all the instincts of my birth and culture of a Christian home set me at antagonism to it at every point.

"This feeling of disgust was often accompanied with fear. At times, violence stalked abroad unchallenged and dark lowering faces skulked about. Even when we felt no personal danger this incubus of savage life all around weighed on our hearts. Thus it was day and night. Even those hours of twilight, which brood with sweet influences over so many lives, bore to us, on the evening air, the weird cadences of the heathen dance or the chill thrill of the war-whoop.

Ours was a serious life. The earnestness of our parents in the pursuit of their work could not fail to impress in some degree the children. The main purpose of Christianizing that people was felt in everything. It was like garrison life in time of war. But this seriousness was not ascetical or moroseful. Far from it. Those missionary heroes were full of gladness. With all the disadvantages of such a childhood was the rich privilege of understanding the meaning of cheerful earnestness in Christian life."

REV. STEPHEN R. RIGGS, D.D., LL.D.,
Forty-five Years a Missionary to the Dakotas.

CHAPTER III.

Isolation.—Strenuous Life.—Formation of Dakota Language Dictionary. —Grammar.— Literature.—Bible Translation.—Massacre.—Fleeing Missionaries.—Blood.—Anglo Saxons Triumph.— Loyal Indians.—Monument.

Thus for more than a quarter of a century, the glorious work of conquering the Sioux nation for Christ went on. It was pushed vigorously at every mission station from Lac-qui-Parle to Red Wing and from Kaposia to Hazelwood. Great progress was made in these years. And such a work!

The workers were buried out of sight of their fellow-white men. Lac-qui-Parle was more remote from Boston than Manilla is today. It took Stephen R. Riggs three months to pass with his New England bride from the green hills of her native state to Fort Snelling. It was a further journey of thirteen days over a trackless trail, through the wilderness, to their mission home on the shores of the Lake-that-speaks. Even as late as 1843, it required a full month's travel for the first bridal tour of Agnes Carson Johnson as Mrs. Robert Hopkins from the plains of Ohio to the prairies of Minnesota. It was no pleasure tour in Pullman palace cars, on palatial limited trains, swiftly speeding over highly polished rails from the far east to the Falls of St. Anthony, in those days. It was a weary, weary pilgrimage of weeks by boat and stage, by private conveyance and oft-times on foot. One can make a tour of Europe today with greater ease and in less time than those isolated workers at Lac-qui-Parle could revisit their old homes in Ohio and New England.

Within their reach was no smithy and no mill until they built one; there was no post office within one hundred miles, and all supplies were carried from Boston to New Orleans by sloops; then by steamboats almost the whole length of the Mississippi; then the flatboat-men sweated and swore as they poled them up the Minnesota to the nearest landing-place; then they had to be hauled overland one hundred and twenty-five miles. These trips were ever attended with heavy toil, often with great suffering and sometimes with loss of life.

Small was the support received from the Board. The entire income of the mission, including government aid to the schools, was less than one thousand dollars a year. Upon this meager sum, three ordained missionaries, two teachers and farmers, and six women, with eight or ten children were maintained. This also, covered travelling expenses, books and printing.

The rude and varied dialects of the different bands of the savage Sioux had been reduced to a written language. This was truly a giant task. It required men who were fine linguists, very studious, patient, persistent, and capable of utilizing their knowledge under grave difficulties. Such *were* the Ponds, Dr. Williamson, Mr. Riggs and Joseph Renville by whom the great task was accomplished. It took months and years of patient, persistent, painstaking efforts; but it was finally accomplished.

In 1852, the Dakota Dictionary and Grammar were published by the Smithsonian Institute at its expense. The dictionary contained sixteen thousand words and received the warm commendation of philologists generally. The language itself is still growing and valuable additions are being made to it year by year.

Within a few years, a revised and greatly enlarged edition should be, and probably will be published for the benefit of the Sioux nation.

The Word of God too, had been translated into this wild, barbaric tongue. This was in truth a mighty undertaking. It involved on the part of the translators a knowledge of the French, Latin, Greek, Hebrew and Sioux tongues and required many years of unremitting toil on the part of those, who wrought out its accomplishment in their humble log cabins on the shores of Lakes Calhoun and Lac-qui-Parle, and at Kaposia and Traverse des Sioux, Yellow Medicine and Hazelwood.

But it, too, was completed and published in 1879, by the American Bible Society. Hymn-books and textbooks had also been prepared and published in the new language. Books like the Pilgrims Progress had been issued in it—a literature for a great nation had been created. Comfortable churches and mission homes had been erected at the various mission stations. Out of the eight thousand Sioux Indians in Minnesota, more than one hundred converts had been gathered into the church. The faithful missionaries, who had toiled so long, with but little encouragement, now looked forward hopefully into the future.

Apparently the time to favor their work had come. But suddenly all their pleasant anticipations vanished—all their high hopes were blasted.

It was August 17, 1862, a lovely Sabbath of the Lord. It was sacramental Sabbath at Hazelwood. As their custom was, that congregation of believers and Yellow Medicine came together to commemorate their Lord's death. The house was well-filled and the missionaries have ever remembered that Sabbath as one of precious interest, for it was the last time they ever assembled in that beautiful little chapel. A great trial of their faith and patience was before them and they knew it not. But the loving Saviour knew that both the missionaries and the native Christians required just such a rest with Him before the terrible trials came upon them.

As the sun sank that day into the bosom of the prairies, a fearful storm of fire and blood burst upon the defenseless settlers and missionaries. Like the dread cyclone, it came, unheralded, and like that much-to-be-dreaded monster of the prairies, it left desolation and death in its pathway. The Sioux arose against the whites and in their savage wrath swept the prairies of Western Minnesota as with a besom of destruction. One thousand settlers perished and hundreds of happy homes were made desolate. The churches, school-houses and homes of the missionaries were laid in ashes. However, all the missionaries and their households escaped safely out of this fiery furnace of barbaric fury to St. Paul and Minneapolis. All else seemed lost beyond the possibility of recovery.

In dismay, the missionaries fled from the wreck of their churches and homes. There were forty persons in that band of fugitives, missionaries and their friends, who spent a week of horrors—never-to-be-forgotten—in their passage over the prairies to St. Paul and Minneapolis. By day they were horrified by the marks of bloody cruelties along their pathway—dead and mangled bodies, wrecked and abandoned homes. At night, they were terrified by the flames of burning homes and fears of the tomahawks and the scalping knives of their cruel foes. The nights were full of fear and dread. Every voice was hushed except to give necessary orders; every eye swept the hills and valleys around; every ear was intensely strained to catch the faintest noise, in momentary expectation of the unearthly war-whoop and of seeing dusky forms with gleaming tomahawks uplifted. In the moonlight mirage of the prairies, every taller clump of grass, every blacker hillock grew into a blood thirsty Indian, just ready to leap upon them. But, by faith, they were able to sing in holy confidence:

> "God is our refuge and our strength;
> In straits a present aid;
> Therefore although the hills remove
> We will not be afraid."

And the God, in whom they trusted, fulfilled his promises to them and brought them all, in safety, to the Twin Cities. And as they passed the boundary line of safety, every heart joined in the glad-song of praise and thanksgiving, which went up to heaven. "Jehovah has triumphed, His people are free," seemed to ring through the air.

Little Crow, the chieftain of the Kaposia Band was the acknowledged leader of the Indian forces in this uprising. He was forty years of age, possessed of considerable military ability; wise in council and brave on the field of battle. He had wrought, in secret, with his fellow-tribesmen, until he had succeeded in the formation of the greatest combination of the Indians against the whites since the days of Tecumseh and the Prophet in the Ohio country, fifty years before. He had under his control a large force of Indian warriors armed with Winchesters; and on the morning of the battle, he mustered on the hills around New Ulm, the largest body of Indian cavalry ever gathered together in America.

MINNEHAHA FALLS.

PERILS BY THE HEATHEN MISSIONARIES FLEEING FROM INDIAN MASSACRE IN 1862.

Thursday morning of that terrible week, after an all-night's rain, found them all cold, wet through and utterly destitute of cooked food and fuel. That noon they came to a clump of trees and camped down on the wet prairies for the rest of the day. They killed a stray cow and made some bread out of flour, salt and water. An artist, one of the company, took the pictures here given.

The whites arose in their might and, under the leadership of that gallant general, Henry H. Sibley, gave battle to their savage foes. Then followed weeks of fierce and bloody warfare. It was no child's play. On the one side were arrayed the fierce warriors of the Sioux nation, fighting for their ancestral homes, their ancient hunting grounds, their deer-parks and the graves of their ancestors. "We *must* drive the white man east of the Mississippi," was the declaration of Little Crow, and he added the savage boast; "We will establish our winter-quarters in St. Paul and Minneapolis." Over against them, were the brave pioneers of Minnesota, battling for the existence of their beloved state, for their homes, and for the lives and honor of their wives and daughters. The thrilling history of the siege of New Ulm, of the battle of Birch Coullie, of Fort Ridgely and Fort Abercrombie, and of other scenes of conflict is written in the mingled blood of the white man, and of the red man on the beautiful plains of western Minnesota. The inevitable result ensued. The Sioux were defeated, large numbers were slain in battle or captured, and in despair, the others fled to the then uninhabited regions beyond the Red River of the North. Many of these found refuge under the British flag in Prince Rupert's Land (now Manitoba).

One of the redeeming features in this terrible tragedy of '62, was the unflinching loyalty of the Christian Sioux to the cause of peace. They stood firmly together against the war-party and for the whites. They abandoned their homes and pitched their teepees closely together. This became the rallying point for all who were opposed to the outbreak. They called it Camp Hope, which was changed after the flight of Little Crow's savage band to Camp Lookout. Two days later, when General Sibley's victorious troops arrived, it was named Camp Release. Then it was that the captives, more than three hundred in number were released, chiefly through the efforts of the Christianized Indians.

In 1902, at the celebration of the fortieth anniversary of the battle of New Ulm, by invitation of the citizens, a band of Sioux Indians pitched their teepees in the public square and participated in the exercises of the occasion. This was a striking illustration of the amity now existing between the two races upon the very ground, where their immediate ancestors so eagerly sought each other's life-blood, in the recent past. Here on the morn of battle, on the surrounding hills, in the long ago, Little Crow had marshalled his fierce warriors, who rushed eagerly in savage glee, again and again, to the determined assault, only to be driven back, by the brave Anglo-Saxon defenders. Tablets, scattered here and there over the plains, in the valley of the Minnesota River, tell the story of the Sioux nation, in the new Northwest.

John Baptiste Renville, a licentiate of the Presbyterian church, and who later was a famous preacher of great power among his own people, remained inside of the Indian lines, and was a powerful factor in causing the counter revolution which hastened the overthrow of the rebellion, and the deliverance of the white captives. Elder Peter Big Fire turned the war party from the trail of the fleeing missionaries and their friends, thus saving two-score lives. One Indian alone, John Other-Day, saved the lives of sixty-two whites. One elder of the church, Simon Anakwangnanne, restored a captive white woman and three children. And still another, Paul Mintakutemanne, rescued a white woman and several children and a whole family of half-breeds. These truly "good Indians" saved the lives of more than their own number of whites,—probably two hundred souls in all.

In token of her appreciation of these invaluable services, Minnesota has caused a monument to be erected in honor of these real braves, on the very plains, then swept by the Sioux with fire and blood, in their savage wrath.

It is located on the battlefield of Birch Coullie, near Morton in Renville County. The cenotaph is built entirely of native stone of different varieties. It rises to the height of fifty-eight feet above the beautiful prairies by which it is surrounded. It bears this appropriate inscription

---

HUMANITY.

Erected A.D. 1899, by the Minnesota Valley Historical Society to commemorate the brave, faithful and humane conduct of the loyal Indians who saved the lives of white people and were true to their obligations throughout the Sioux war in Minnesota in 1862, and especially to honor the services of those here named:

       Other Day—Ampatutoricna.
       Paul—Mintakutemanne.
       Lorenzo Lawrence—Towanctaton.
       Simon—Anakwangnanne.
       Mary Crooks—Mankahta Heita-win.

CHAPTER IV.

Prisoners in Chains.—Executions.—Pentecost in Prison.—Three Hundred Baptisms.— Church Organized.—Sacramental Supper.—Prison Camp.—John P. Williamson.—One Hundred Converts.—Davenport.—Release.—Niobrara. —Pilgrim Church.

"Who are these that fly as a cloud, and as the doves to their windows?" —*Isaiah 60:8.*

But now occurred the strangest phase of this wondrously strange story. In November, 1862, four hundred defeated Indian warriors, many of them leaders of their people, were confined in prison-pens at Mankato, Minnesota. While free on the prairies, these wild warriors had bitterly hated the missionaries with all the intensity of their savage natures. They had vigorously opposed every effort of the missionaries in their behalf. They had scornfully rejected the invitations of the Gospel. But now in their claims, they earnestly desired to hear the glad tidings they had formerly scorned. They sent for the missionaries to visit them in prison and the missionaries responded with eager joy. And the Holy Spirit accompanied them. Thirty-eight of the prisoners were under the death-sentence and were executed in December.

"I remember," said Dr. Williamson, "feeling a great desire to preach to them, mingled with a kind of terror partly from a sense of grave responsibility in speaking to so many whose probation was so nearly closed, and partly from a sense of fear of hearing them say to me "Go home; when we were free we would not hear you preach to us; why do you come here to torment us when we are in chains and cannot go away." It was a great relief to find them listening intently to all I had to say."

The prisoners were supplied with Bibles and other books, and for a time, the prison became a school. They were all eager to learn. The more their minds were directed to God and His Word, the more they became interested in secular studies.

Very soon the Indians of their own accord began holding meetings every morning and evening in which they sang and spoke and prayed. In a short time, there were ninety converts that would lead in public prayer. Of those who were executed, thirty were baptized. Standing in a foot of snow, manacled two and two, they frequently gathered to sing and pray and listen to the words of eternal life. Of this work, the Rev. Gideon H. Pond wrote at the time; "There is a degree of religious interest manifested by them, which is incredible. They huddle themselves together every morning and evening, read the scriptures, sing hymns, confess one to another and pray together. They declare they have left their superstitions forever, and that they do and will embrace the religion of Jesus."

In March, Mr. Pond visited Mankato again and spent two Sabbaths with the men in prison, establishing them in their new faith. Before his departure, he administered the Lord's supper, to these new converts. And again the Mankato prison-pens witnessed a strange and wondrous scene. Three hundred embittered, defeated Indian warriors, manacled, fettered with balls and chains,—but clothed and in their right minds,—were sitting in groups upon the wintry grounds reverently observing the Lord's supper. Elders Robert Hopkins, Peter Big-Fire and David Grey Cloud officiated with reverence and dignity. The whole movement was marvelous! It was like a "nation born in a day." And after many years of severe testing, all who know the facts, testify that it was a genuine work of God's Holy Spirit. The massacre and the subsequent events destroyed the power of the Priests of Devils, which had previously ruled and ruined these wretches' tribes. They themselves, exploded the dynamite under the throne of Paganism and shattered it to fragments forever.

In 1863, these Indians were transferred to Davenport, Iowa, where they were confined in prison for three years. In 1866 they were released by the government and returned to their native prairies, where they then became the nuclei of other churches, other Sabbath schools and other church organizations; and so these formerly savage Sioux became a benediction rather than a terror to their neighbors on the plains of the Dakotas. The church of the prison-pen became the prolific mother of churches.

While these events were transpiring in the prison-pen at Mankato, a similar work of grace was also in progress in the prison camp at Fort Snelling, where fifteen hundred men, women and children, mainly the families of the Mankato prisoners, were confined under guard. The conditions, in both places, were very similar. In the camp as well as in the prison, they were in grave troubles and great anxieties. In their distresses they called mightily upon the Lord. Here John, the Beloved (John P. Williamson D.D.) ministered to their temporal and spiritual wants. The Lord heard and answered their burning and agonizing cries. By gradual steps, but with overwhelming power came the heavenly visitation. Many were convicted; confessions and professions were made; idols reverenced for many generations were thrown away by the score. More than one hundred and twenty were baptized and organized into a Presbyterian church, which, after years of bitter wandering, was united with the church of the Prison Pen and formed the large congregation of the Pilgrim church.

Thus all that winter long, '62-3, there was in progress within the rude walls of those terrible prison-pens at Mankato, one of the most wonderful revivals since the day of Pentecost. And in February, '63, Dr. Williamson and Rev. Gideon H. Pond spent a week in special services amongst them.

The most careful examinations possible were made into their individual spiritual condition and the most faithful instruction given them as to their Christian duties; then those Indian warriors were all baptized, received into the communion of the church and organized into a Presbyterian church within the walls of the stockade; *three hundred in a day!* Truly impressive was

THE BAPTISMAL SCENE.

The conditions of baptism were made very plain to the prisoners and it was offered to only such as were willing to comply fully with those conditions. All were forbidden to receive the rite, who did not do it heartily to the God of Heaven, whose eye penetrated each of their hearts. All, by an apparently hearty response, indicated their desire to receive the rite on the proffered conditions. As soon as the arrangements were completed, they came forward one by one, as their names were called and were baptized into the name of the Father, Son and Holy Spirit, while each subject stood with the right hand raised and head bowed and many of them with their eyes closed with an appearance of profound reverence. As each came forward to be baptized one of the ministers addressed to him in a low voice a few appropriate words. This was the substance of these personal addresses. "My brother, this is a mark of God, which is placed upon you. You will carry it with you while you live. It introduces you into the great family of God who looks down from heaven, not upon your head but into your heart. This ends your superstition, and from this time you are to call God your Father. Remember to honor Him. Be resolved to do His will." Each one responded heartily, "Yes, I will."

Gideon H. Pond then addressed them collectively.

"Hitherto I have addressed you as friends; now I call you brethren. For years we have contended together on this subject of religion; now our contentions cease. We have one Father, we are one family. I shall soon leave you and shall probably see your faces no more in this world. Your adherence to the medicine sack and the Natawe (consecrated war weapons) have brought you to your ruin. The Lord Jesus Christ can save you. Seek him with all your heart. He looks not upon your heads nor on your lips but into your bosoms. Brothers, I will make use of a term of brotherly salutation, to which you have been accustomed to your medicine dances and say to you: "'Brethren I spread my hands over you and bless you.'"" Three hundred voices responded heartily, "'Amen, yea and Amen.'"

CHAPTER V.

It was 1884. Fifty years since the coming of the Pond brothers to Fort Snelling—twenty-one years since the organization of the church in the prison-pen at Mankato. One bright September day, from the heights of Sisseton, South Dakota, a strangely beautiful scene was spread out before the eye. In the distance the waters of Lake Traverse (source of the Red River of the North), and Big Stone Lake (head waters of the Minnesota), glistened in the bright sunshine, their waters almost commingling ere they began their diverse journeyings—the former to Hudson's Bay, the latter to the Gulf of Mexico. At our feet were prairies rich as the garden of the Lord. The spot was Iyakaptapte, that is the Ascension. Half-way up was a large wooden building, nestling in a grassy cove. Round about on the hillsides were white teepees. Dusky forms were passing to and fro and pressing round the doors and windows. We descended and found ourselves in the midst of a throng of Sioux Indians. Instinctively we asked ourselves, Why are they here? Is this one of their old pagan festivals? Or is it a council of war? We entered. The spacious house was densely packed; we pressed our way to the front. Hark! They are singing. We could not understand the words, but the air was familiar. It was Bishop Heber's hymn (in the Indian tongue):

> "From Greenlands icy mountains,
> From India's coral strand.
>
> * * *
>
> Salvation! O Salvation!
> The joyful sound proclaim,
> Till each remotest nation
> Has learned Messiah's Name.
> Waft, waft, ye winds, His story,
> And you, ye waters, roll,
> Till like a sea of glory
> It spreads from pole to pole."

With what joyful emphasis, this strange congregation sang these words.

We breathed easier. This was no pagan festival, no savage council of war. It was the fifteenth grand annual council of the Dakota Christian Indians of the Northwest.

The singing was no weaklunged performance—not altogether harmonious, but vastly sweeter than a war-whoop; certainly hearty and sincere and doubtless an acceptable offering of praise. The Rev. John Baptiste Renville was the preacher. His theme was Ezekiel's vision of the Valley of Dry Bones. We did not knew how he handled his subject. But the ready utterance, the sweet flow of words, the simple earnestness of the speaker and the fixed attention of the audience marked it as a complete success. When the sermon was finished, there was another loud-voiced hymn and then the Council of Days was declared duly opened.

Thus they gather themselves together, year by year to take counsel in reference to the things of the kingdom. The Indian moderator, Artemas Ehnamane, the Santee pastor, was a famous paddle-man, a mighty hunter and the son of a great conjuror and war-prophet, but withal a tender, faithful, spiritual pastor of his people. Rev. Alfred L. Riggs, D.D., the white moderator, who talked so glibly alternately in Sioux and English and smiled so sweetly in both languages at once, was "Good Bird," one of the first white babes born at Lac-qui-Parle. John, The Beloved, one of the chief white workers, as a boy had the site of Minneapolis and St. Paul for a play-ground, and the little Indian lads for his playmates. That week we spent at Iyakaptapte was a series of rich, rare treats. We listened to the theological class of young men, students of Santee and Sisseton. We watched the smiling faces of the women as they bowed in prayer, and brought their offerings to the missionary meetings. Such wondrous liberality those dark-faced sisters displayed. We marked with wonder the intense interest manifested hour by hour by all classes in the sermons, addresses, and especially in the discussion: "How shall we build up the church?" Elder David Grey Cloud said, "We must care for the church if we would make it effective. We must care for all we gather into the church." The Rev. James Red-Wing added, "The work of the church is heavy. When a Red River cart sticks in the mud we call all the help we can and together we lift it out; we must all lift the heavy load of the church." The Rev. David Grey Cloud closed with: "We must cast out all enmity, have love for one another and then we shall be strong."

"Does the keeping of Dakota customs benefit or injure the Dakota People?"

Deacon Boy-that-walks-on-the-water responded emphatically. "The ancient Dakota customs are all bad. There is no good in them. They are all sin, all sorrow. All medicine men are frauds. Jesus is the only one to hold to." Rev. Little-Iron-Thunder said "When I was a boy I was taught the sacred dances and all the mysteries; to shoot with the bag; to hold the sacred shell. To gain a name, the Dakotas will suffer hunger, cold, even death. But all this is a cheat. It will not give life to the people. Only one name will give life, — even Jesus." Rev. Daniel Renville declared: "Faith is the thing our people need; not faith in everything, but faith in Christ; not for hope of reward."

There were evening gatherings in the interest of the Young Men's Christian Associations and the Young People's Christian Endeavor Societies. These are two of the most hopeful features of the work. With the young men and maidens of the tribe in careful training in Christian knowledge and for Christian service, there must be far-reaching and permanent beneficent results.

Sabbath came! A glorious day! A fitting crown of glory for a week of such rare surprises. A strange chanting voice, like that of a herald mingled with our day-break dreams. Had we been among the Moslems, we should have thought it the muezzin's cry. It was all Indian to us, but it was indeed a call to prayer with this translation in English:—

"Morning is coming! Morning is coming! Wake up! Wake up! Come to sing! Come to pray."

Very soon, the sweet music of prayer and praise from the white teepees on the hillside, rose sweetly on the air, telling us that the day of their glad solemnities had begun. The great congregation assembled in the open air. Pastor Renville, who as a little lad played at the feet of the translators of the Bible into the Sioux language, and who as a young man organized a counter revolution among the Christian Indians in favor of the government in the terrible days of '62, presided with dignity, baptizing a little babe and receiving several recent converts into the church. A man of rare powers and sweet temperament is the Rev. John Baptiste Renville, youngest son of the famous Joseph Renville. A wonderfully strange gathering is this. Hundreds of Indians seated in semi-circles on the grass, reverently observing the Lord's Supper. Probably one-third of the males in that assemblage were participants in the bloody wars of the Sioux nation. The sermon was delivered by Solomon His-Own-Grandfather, who had taken an active part in the war of 1862, but was now a missionary among his own people in Manitoba. The bread was broken by Artemas Ehnamane ("Walking Along"), who was condemned and pardoned, and then converted after that appalling tragedy in 1862. The wine was poured by the man whom all the Sioux lovingly call John (Dr. John P. Williamson) who led them in the burning revival scenes in the prison-camp at Fort Snelling in 1863. And as he referred to those thrilling times, their tears flowed like rain. It is said that Indians cannot weep, but scores of them wept that day at Ascension. One of the officiating elders was a son of the notorious chieftain Little Crow, who was so prominent against the Anglo-Saxons in those days of carnage. As we partook of those visible symbols of our Saviour's broken body, and shed blood, with this peculiar congregation, so recently accustomed to the war-whoop and the scalp-dance, we freely mingled our tears with theirs. And as our minds ranged over the vast Dakota field and as we remembered the thousands of Christian Sioux, their Presbytery and their Association, their scores of churches and their many Sabbath Schools, their Y.M.C.A. and their Y.P.S.C.E. associations, their missionary societies and other beneficent organizations, their farms and homes, their present pure, happy condition, and contrasted it with their former superstition, nakedness and filthy teepee life, we sang joyfully;

> Behold! What wondrous works
> Have, by the Lord, been wrought;
> Behold! What precious souls
> Have, by His blood, been bought.

As the shades of evening drew on, the different bands held their farewell meetings in their teepees. There were sounds of sweet music—joyous ones—echoing and re-echoing over the prairies—"He leadeth me, Oh precious thought," "Nearer, my God to thee," "Blessed Assurance, Jesus hath given"—until the whole was blended in one grand refrain:—

> "Blest be the tie that binds
> Our hearts in Christian love;
> The fellowship of Christian minds
> Is like to that above."

The Council Tent was in darkness! The lights were out in the teepees. The whole camp was wrapped in solid slumber. And as we sunk to rest in our bed of new-mown hay, we breathed a prayer for the slumbering Sioux around us; May the Cloud, by day, and the Pillar of Fire, by night, guide the Sioux Nation through the Red Sea of Savagery, superstition and sin to the Promised Land of Christian Civilization.

THE NATIVE MISSIONARY SOCIETY.

It is well worth a journey to the land of the Dakotas to witness an anniversary gathering of their Woman's Missionary Society. You enter the great Council Tent. It is thronged with these nut-brown women of the plains. A matronly woman welcomes you, and presides with grace and dignity. A bright and beautiful young maiden—a graduate of Santee or Good Will—controls the organ and sweetly leads the service of song. And oh how they do sing! You cannot understand the words, but the airs are familiar. Now it is Bishop Coxe's "Latter Day" sung with vim in the Indian tongue;

> "We are living, we are dwelling,
> In a grand and awful time;
> In an age on ages telling,
> To be living is sublime."

And now some sedate matron rises and reads a carefully written paper, contrasting their past, vile teepee life of ignoble servitude to Satan, with their present, pure life of glorious liberty in the Lord Jesus Christ. And then they sing, so earnestly for they are thinking of their pagan sisters of the wild tribes, sitting in darkness and the shadow of death, in the regions beyond. The hymn is Draper's "Missionary Chant."

> "Ye Christian heralds, go proclaim
> Salvation through Emmanuel's name;
> To distant lands the tidings bear
> And plant the Rose of Sharon there."

And now a lively young lass, neatly attired, comes forward and with a fine, clear accent, recites a poem of hope, touching the bright future of their tribe, when the present generation of young men and maidens, nourished in Christian homes, educated in Christian schools and trained in the Young People's societies for efficient service, shall control their tribe, and move the great masses of their people upward and God-ward, and elevate the Sioux Nation to a lofty plane of Christian civilization and culture; and enable them to display to the world the rich fruition of Christian service. And, by request, their voices ring out in song these thrilling words;

> "Watchman, tell us of the night,
> For the morning seems to dawn;
> Traveller, darkness takes its flight,
> Doubt and terror are withdrawn.
> Watchman, let thy wanderings cease;
> Hie thee, to thy quiet home;
> Traveller, lo, the Prince of Peace,
> Lo, the Son of God is come!"

Fervent prayers are frequently interspersed in these exercises. And oh, what wondrous liberality these dark-skinned sisters of the Dakota plains display!

How full their hands are with rich gifts, gleaned out of their poverty for the treasury of their Saviour-King. For many years, the average annual contributions per capita to missions, by these Sioux sisters, have fully measured up to the standard of their more highly favored Anglo-Saxon sisters of the wealthy Presbyterian and Congregational denominations, of which they form a humble part.

CHAPTER VI.

1905—Sisseton.—John Baptiste Renville.—Presbytery of Dakota.

It was 1905. From the heights of Sisseton, South Dakota, another striking scene met the eye. The great triangular Sisseton reserve of one million acres no longer exists. Three hundred thousand of its choicest acres are now held in severalty by the fifteen hundred members of the Sisseton and Wahpeton Band of the Dakotas—the "Leaf Dwellers" of the plains. Their homes, their schools, their churches cover the prairies. That spire pointing heavenward rises from Good Will Church, a commodious, well-furnished edifice, with windows of stained glass. Within its walls, there worship on the Sabbath, scores of dusky Presbyterian Christians. The pastor, the Rev. Charles Crawford, in whose veins there flows the mingled blood of the shrewd Scotch fur trader and the savage Sioux, lives in that comfortable farm house a few rods distant. He has a pastorate that many a white minister might covet. Miles to the west, still stands in its grassy cove on the coteaux of the prairie, the Church of the Ascension, referring not to the ascension of our Lord, but to "the going up" of the prairies. On the hill above it, is the cozy home of the pastor emeritus, the Rev. John Baptiste Renville, whose pastorate, in point of continuous service, has been the longest in the two Dakotas. After a long lifetime of faithful ministrations to the people of his own charge, enfeebled by age and disease, he sweetly fell asleep in Jesus, Dec. 19, 1904. Doubtless his is a starry crown, richly gemmed, in token of the multitude of the souls of his fellow tribesmen, led to the Savior by his tender, faithful ministry of a life-time in their midst. Round about these two churches cluster half a dozen other congregations, worshipping in comfortable church homes. These form only a part of the

PRESBYTERY OF DAKOTA.

The original Presbytery of Dakota was organized September 30, 1844, at the mission Home of Dr. Williamson, at Lac-qui-Parle, Minnesota. It was organized, by the missionaries, among the Dakotas, for the furtherance of their peculiar work. The charter members were three ministers, the Rev. Samuel W. Pond, Rev. Thomas S. Williamson, M.D., and Rev. Stephen R. Riggs and one elder Alexander G. Huggins. It was an independent presbytery, and, for fourteen years, was not connected with any Synod. It was a lone presbytery, in a vast region, now covered by a dozen Synods and scores of presbyteries. For many years, the white and Indian churches that were organized in Minnesota, were united in this presbytery and wrought harmoniously together. In 1858, the General Assembly of Presbyterian churches (N.S.) invited this independent presbytery to unite with her two Minnesota Presbyteries and form the Synod of Minnesota which was accomplished.

Solely on account of the barrier of the language, the missionaries and churches among the Dakotas, petitioned the Synod of Minnesota to organize them into a separate presbytery. And the Synod so ordered and it was so done, September 30, 1867, just twenty-three years after the first organization at Lac-qui-Parle. By this order, the limits of the Presbytery of Dakota became the churches and ministers among the Dakota Indians. It is the only Presbytery in existence, without any geographical boundaries. At present, there are seventeen ordained Indian ministers upon the roll of this presbytery—workmen of whom neither they themselves nor any others have any cause to be ashamed. There are, also, under its care, twenty-eight well-organized churches, aggregating more than fifteen hundred communicants, and eight hundred Sabbath-School members. The contributions of these fifteen hundred Dakota Presbyterians in 1904, exceeded the sum of six thousand dollars for all religious purposes.

Among the "Dispersed" of the Sioux nation, in Manitoba, there is one organized Presbyterian church of twenty-five communicant members. It is the church of Beulah and is in connection with the Presbyterian church of Canada.

In all, twenty-one Sioux Indians have been ordained to the Presbyterian ministry, by the Presbytery of Dakota. Of these, Artemas Ehnamane, Titus Icaduze, Joseph Iron Door, and John Baptiste Renville have all passed on, from the beautiful prairies of the Dakotas, to the celestial plains of glory. And how warm must have been their greeting as they passed through the pearly gates of the city, whose builder and maker is God. Gideon Pond, Dr. Williamson, Samuel W. Pond, Stephen R. Riggs and Robert Hopkins, Margaret Williamson, Mary Riggs and Aunt Jane and other faithful missionaries and thousands of redeemed Dakotas, welcomed them, with glad hozannas, and sweet are the songs they sing as they walk together, under the trees, on the banks of the River of Life.

The Dakota Congregational association has under its care thirteen organized churches, with more than one thousand communicants and one thousand Sabbath school members. The prominent leaders of its work are Alfred L. Riggs D.D., of Santee, Nebraska, and Rev. Thomas L. Riggs of Oahe, South Dakota. They are the worthy sons of their famous father, Stephen R. Riggs, D.D., one of the heroic pioneers in the Dakota work. The native ministers are Francis Frazier, Edwin Phelps, James Garvie, James Wakutamani and Elias Gilbert. This association is a mighty factor in God's plan, for the upbuilding of the Dakotas, in the things that are noble and of good report.

The Presbyterian and Congregationalists have wrought together, side by side, for seventy years, in this glorious enterprise. Under their auspices, forty-four churches, many schools and other beneficent organizations are in efficient operation among these former savage dwellers on these plains.

Seven other natives have, also, been ordained to the priesthood in the Episcopal Church, making thirty-three in all, who have served their fellow-tribesmen in the high and holy office of the Christian ministry. There is not a single ordained Romish priest among the Sioux Indians.

"Watchman, tell us of the night,

What its signs of promise are."

Seventy years ago, among the twenty-five thousand Sioux Indians in the United States, there was not a single church, not even one professing Christian.

They were all polytheistic pagans. There were signs of pagan worship about every teepee. It might be the medicine sack tied behind the conical wigwam, or a yard of broadcloth, floating from the top of a flagpole as a sacrifice to some deity. There was more or less idol-worship in all their gatherings. One of the simplest forms was the holding of a well-filled pipe at arm's length, with the mouth-piece upward, while the performers said, "O Lord, take a smoke and have mercy on me." In the feasts and dances, the forms were more elaborate. The Sun-dance continued for days of fasting and sacrificial work by the participants.

Now these signs of pagan worship have almost entirely disappeared among the Dakotas. These facts speak volumes—one in eight of the Dakotas is a Presbyterian. There are two-thirds as many Congregationalists, twice as many Episcopalians and twice as many Catholics. More than one-half of the Dakotas have been baptized in the name of the Triune God and thousands of them are professed followers of the Lord Jesus Christ.

Now what has wrought this great change among the Dakotas? It was the power of the Holy Spirit of the Lord, working through the means of grace as employed and applied by these faithful missionaries. They renounced heathenism, not because the government so ordered, but because they found that there was no God like Jehovah and Jehovah said, "Thou shalt have no other gods before me." Even those who have not accepted Christ have generally cast away their idols.

Now do missions pay? Do Indian missions pay? Let the grand work among the Dakotas and its glorious results be an all sufficient answer. It does pay a thousand fold.

Hear the Christian tribesmen sing the Hymn of the Sioux.

> Lift aloft the starry banner,
> Let it wave o'er land and sea;
> Shout aloud and sing hosanna!
> Praise the Lord, who set us free!
> Here we stand amazed and wonder
> Such a happy change to see;
> The bonds of sin are burst asunder!
> Praise the Lord who set us free.
> Long we lay in darkness pining,
> Not a ray of hope had we!
> Now the Gospel Sun is shining:
> Praise the Lord who set us free.
> In one loud and joyful chorus,
> Heart and soul now join will we;
> Salvation's Sun is shining o'er us!
> Praise the Lord who set us free.

PART II.
SOME SIOUX STORIETTES.

CHAPTER I.

The Dead Papoose.—The Maiden's Feast.

THE DEAD PAPOOSE.

The Indian mother, when her child dies, does not believe that swift angels bear it into the glorious sunshine of the spirit-land; but she has a beautiful dream to solace her bereavement. The cruel empty places, which everywhere meet the eye of the weeping white mother, are unknown to her, for to her tender fancy a little spirit-child fills them.

It is not a rare sight to see a pair of elaborate tiny moccasins above a little Indian grave. A mother's fingers have embroidered them, a mother's hand has hung them there, to help the baby's feet over the long rough road that stretches between his father's wigwam and the Great Chief's happy hunting grounds.

Indians believe that a baby's spirit cannot reach the spirit-land until the child, if living, would have been old enough and strong enough to walk. Until that time the little spirit hovers about its mother. And often it grows tired—oh so very tired! So the tender mother carries a papoose's cradle on her back that the baby spirit may ride and rest when it will. The cradle is filled with the softest feathers, for the spirit rests more comfortably upon soft things—hard things bruise it—and all the papoose's old toys dangle from the crib, for the dead papoose may love to play even as the living papoose did.

THE MAIDENS' FEAST.

Of the many peculiar customs of the Indians in the long ago, perhaps the most unique was the annual "feast of Maidens." One was given at Fort Ellis, Manitoba, some thirty years ago, in a natural amphitheatre, surrounded by groves, fully one thousand feet above the Assiniboine River.

It was observed at a reunion of the Sioux, and of the Assiniboines and the Crees, three friendly tribes.

In his "Indian Boyhood," that brilliant Sioux author, Dr. Charles Alexander Eastman, great-grandson of Cloudman or Man-of-the-sky, that potential friend of the missionaries in pioneer days at Lake Calhoun, graphically describes it thus:—

"One bright summer morning, while we were still at our meal of jerked buffalo meat, we heard the herald of the Wahpeton band upon his calico pony as he rode round our circle.

"White Eagle's daughter, the maiden Red Star, invites all the maidens of all the tribes to come and partake of her feast. It will be in the Wahpeton Camp, before the sun reaches the middle of the sky. All pure maidens are invited. Red Star, also, invites the young men to be present, to see that no unworthy maiden should join in the feast."

The herald soon completed the rounds of the different camps, and it was not long before the girls began to gather. It was regarded as a semi-sacred feast.

It would be desecration for any to attend, who was not perfectly virtuous. Hence it was regarded as an opportune time for the young men to satisfy themselves as to who were the virtuous maids of the tribe.

There were apt to be surprises before the end of the day. Any young man was permitted to challenge any maiden, whom he knew to be untrue. But woe to him, who could not prove his case. It meant little short of death to the man, who endeavored to disgrace a woman without cause.

From the various camps, the girls came singly or in groups, dressed in bright colored calicoes or in heavily fringed and beaded buckskin. Their smooth cheeks and the center of their glossy hair was touched with vermillion. All brought with them wooden basins to eat from. Some who came from a considerable distance were mounted upon ponies; a few for company or novelty's sake rode double.

The maidens' circle was formed about a cone-shaped rock, which stood upon its base. This was painted red. Beside it, two new arrows were lightly stuck into the ground. This is a sort of altar, to which each maiden comes before taking her assigned place in the circle, and lightly touches first the stone and then the arrows. By this oath, she declares her purity. Whenever a girl approaches the altar there is a stir among the spectators and sometimes a rude youth would call out; "Take care! you will overturn the rock or pull out the arrows!"

Immediately behind the maidens' circle is the chaperons' circle. This second circle is almost as interesting to look at as the inner one.

The old women watched every movement of their respective charges with the utmost concern. There was never a more gorgeous assembly of its kind than this one. The day was perfect. The Crees, displaying their characteristic horsemanship, came in groups; the Assiniboines with their curious pompadour well covered with red paint. The various bands of Sioux all carefully observed the traditional peculiarities of dress and behavior.

The whole population of the region had assembled and the maidens came shyly into the circle. During the simple preparatory rites, there was a stir of excitement among a group of Wahpeton Sioux young men. All the maidens glanced nervously toward the scene of the disturbance. Soon a tall youth emerged from the throng of spectators and advanced toward the circle. With a steady step, he passed by the chaperons, and approached the maidens' circle.

At last, he stopped behind a pretty Assiniboine maiden of good family and said:

"I am sorry, but according to custom, you should not be here."

The girl arose in confusion, but she soon recovered her control.

"What do you mean?" she demanded indignantly. "Three times you have come to court me, but each time I have refused to listen to you. I have turned my back upon you. Twice I was with Washtinna. She can tell the people that this is true. The third time I had gone for water when you intercepted me and begged me to stop and listen. I refused because I did not know you. My chaperon Makatopa-wee knows I was gone but a few minutes. I never saw you anywhere else."

The young man was unable to answer this unmistakable statement of facts and it became apparent that he had sought to revenge himself for her repulse.

"Woo! Woo! Carry him out!" was the order of the Chief of the Indian police, and the audacious youth was hurried away into the nearest ravine to be chastised.

The young woman who had thus established her good name returned to the circle and the feast was served. The "maidens' song" was sung, and four times they danced in a ring around the altar.

Each maid, as she departed, took her oath to remain pure until she should meet her husband.

CHAPTER II.

GRANDMOTHER POND.

Grandmother Pond is one of the rarest spirits, one of the loveliest characters in Minnesota. She is the last living link between the past and the present—between that heroic band of pioneer missionaries who came to Minnesota prior to 1844, and those who joined the ranks of this glorious missionary service in more recent years. Her life reads like a romance.

Agnes Carson Johnson Pond is a native of Ohio—born at Greenfield in 1825. She was the daughter of William Johnson, a physician and surgeon of Chillicothe, Ohio. By the death of her father she was left an orphan at five years of age. Her mother married a worthy minister of the Associate Reformed Presbyterian church, Rev. John McDill. She had superior educational and social advantages and made good use of all her opportunities. She was educated at a seminary at South Hanover, Indiana. There she met her future husband, Robert Hopkins. He, as well as she, was in training for service on mission fields. They were married in 1843. He had already been appointed as a missionary teacher for the Sioux Indians. The young wife was compelled to make her bridal tour in the company of strangers, by boat and stage and private conveyance from Ohio to the then unknown land of the upper Mississippi. It required thirty days then, instead of thirty hours, as now, to pass from Ohio to the Falls of St. Anthony. The bride-groom drove his own team from Galena, Illinois, to Fort Snelling.

HER HUSBAND DROWNED.

Mr. and Mrs. Hopkins were first stationed at Lac-qui-Parle. After one year they were transferred to Traverse des Sioux, near the present site of St. Peter, Minnesota. Here they gave seven years of the most faithful, devoted, self-sacrificing toil for the lost and degraded savages around them. They built a humble home and established and maintained a mission school. Five children were born to them there. Two of these were early called to the celestial home on high. Their life at Traverse des Sioux was a strenuous, isolated, but a fruitful and happy one. It was destined, however, to a speedy and tragic end.

Early in the morning of July 4, 1851, Mr. Hopkins entered the river for a bath. He was never seen alive again. A treacherous swirl in the water at that point suddenly carried him to his death. His wife waited long the carefully prepared morning meal, but her beloved came not again. He went up through the great flood of waters from arduous service on the banks of the beautiful Minnesota to his glorious rewards on the banks of the still more beautiful River of Life.

GRANDMOTHER POND,

The Last Living Member of the Heroic Band of Pioneer Missionaries to the Dakotas, in the 81st Year of Her Age.

Broken-hearted, the young wife, only twenty-six years of age, laid him to rest on the banks of the river whose treacherous waves had robbed her of her life companion. Sadly she closed her home in Minnesota and, with her three little fatherless children, returned to her old home in far-distant Ohio.

Rev. Robert Hopkins enjoyed the full confidence of his colleagues and was greatly beloved by the Indians. His untimely death was an irreparable loss to the mission work among the Sioux.

SECOND BRIDAL TOUR TO THE WEST.

Shortly after the tragedy at Traverse des Sioux, Mrs. Sarah Poage Pond, wife of Rev. Gideon H. Pond, died at Oak Grove Mission of consumption. In 1854 Mr. Pond visited Ohio, where he and Mrs. Hopkins were united in marriage. She made a second bridal tour from Ohio to Minnesota, and toiled by his side till his death in 1878.

In every relation in life in which she has been placed, Mrs. Pond has excelled. While she long ago ceased from active service in mission fields, she ever has been, and still is untiring in her efforts to do good to all as she has opportunity. She is strong and vigorous at the age of eighty. She still resides at the Oak Grove Mission house, her home since 1857, universally beloved and regarded as the best woman in the world by about one hundred descendants.

JOHN P. WILLIAMSON, D.D.,

Superintendent of Presbyterian Sioux Missions.
Forty-five years a missionary to the Sioux.

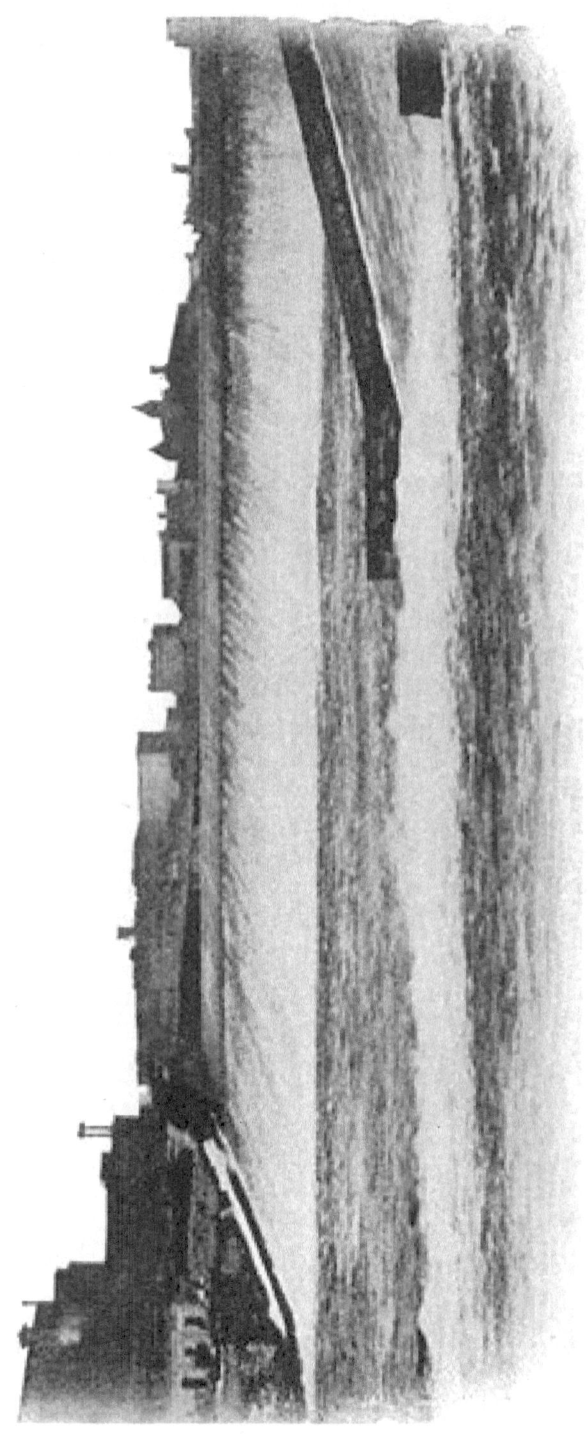

ST. ANTHONY FALLS.

OAK GROVE MISSION HOUSE.

This old land mark is located in Hennepin County, Minnesota, twelve miles southwest of Minneapolis. Here in 1843, Gilbert H. Pond established his headquarters as a missionary to the Sioux Indians. He erected a large log building in which he resided, taught school and preached the gospel. Here, in 1848, the Presbytery of Dakota convened, and ordained Mr. Pond and Robert Hopkins to the Presbyterian ministry. For many years it was the sole source of social, moral, and spiritual light for a wide region for both races. It was also the favorite gathering place of the Indians for sport. In 1852, a great game of ball was played here. Good Road and Grey Iron joined their followers with Cloudman's band of Lake Calhoun in opposition to Little Six and his band from Shakopay. Two hundred and fifty men and boys participated in the game, while two hundred and fifty others were deeply interested spectators. The game lasted for three days and was won by Cloudman and his allies. Forty-six hundred dollars in ponies, blankets and other such property changed hands on the results.

In 1856, the present commodious residence was erected of brick manufactured on the premises. For twenty-one years it was the residence of Rev. Gideon Hollister Pond. He was for twenty years, also, pastor of the white Presbyterian church of Oak Grove. He was a member of the first territorial legislature; the editor of the "The Dakota Friend" the first religious journal published in the state, and he was also the first preacher of the gospel in the city of Minneapolis.

In whatever position he was placed in life, he ever proved himself to be a wise, conscientious, consecrated Christian gentleman. None knew him, but to love him; none knew him, but to praise. He was born in Connecticut, June thirtieth, 1810, and on the twentieth of January, 1878, he passed from his Oak Grove Mission Home through the gates of the celestial city, to go no more out. They laid him to rest in the midst of the people, whom he had loved and served so well for four and forty years and by whom he was universally beloved and admired. None were more sincere in their demonstrations of sorrow than the little company of Dakotas to whom he had been a more than father.

CHAPTER III.

ANPETUSAPAWIN.

A Legend of St. Anthony Falls.

Anpetuzapawin. — A Legend of St Anthony Falls.

> Long ere the white man's bark had seen
> These flower-decked prairies, fair and wide,
> Long ere the white man's bark had been
> Borne on the Mississippi's tide,
> So long ago, Dakotas say,
> Anpetusapawin was born,
> Her eyes beheld these scenes so gay
> First opening on life's rosy morn.

—S. W. Pond.

In the long ago, a young Indian brave espoused as his wife this Indian maiden of whom the poet sings. With her he lived happily for a few years, in the enjoyment of every comfort of which a savage life is capable. To crown their happiness, they were blessed with two lovely children on whom they doted. During this time, by a dint of activity and perseverance in the chase, he became signalized in an eminent degree as a hunter, having met with unrivaled success in the pursuit and capture of the wild denizens of the forest. This circumstance contributed to raise him high in the estimation of his fellow savages and drew a crowd of admiring friends around. This operated as a spur to his ambitions.

At length some of his newly acquired friends suggested to him the propriety of taking another wife, as it would be impossible for one woman to manage the affairs of his household and properly wait upon the many guests his rising importance would call to visit him. They intimated to him that in all probability he would soon be elevated to the chieftainship. His vanity was fired by the suggestion. He yielded readily and accepted a wife they had already selected for him.

After his second marriage, he sought to take his new wife home and reconcile his first wife to the match in the most delicate manner possible. To this end he returned to his first wife, as yet ignorant of what had occurred, and endeavored, by dissimulation, to secure her approval.

"You know," said he, "I can love no one as I love you; yet I see your labors are too great for your powers of endurance. Your duties are daily becoming more and more numerous and burdensome. This grieves me sorely. But I know of only one remedy by which you can be relieved. These considerations constrain me to take another wife. This wife shall be under your control in every respect and ever second to you in my affections." She listened to his narrative in painful anxiety and endeavored to reclaim him from his wicked purpose, refuting all his sophistry by expressions of her unaffected conjugal affection. He left her to meditate. She became more industrious and treated him more tenderly than before. She tried every means in her power to dissuade him from the execution of his vile purpose. She pleaded all the endearments of their former happy life, the regard he had for her happiness and that of the offspring of their mutual love to prevail on him to relinquish the idea of marrying another wife. He then informed her of the fact of his marriage and stated that compliance on her part would be actually necessary. She must receive the new wife into their home. She was determined, however, not to be the passive dupe of his duplicity. With her two children she returned to her parental teepee. In the autumn she joined her friends and kinsmen in an expedition up the Mississippi and spent the winter in hunting. In the springtime, as they were returning, laden with peltries, she and her children occupied a canoe by themselves. On nearing the Falls of St. Anthony she lingered in the rear till the others had landed a little above the falls.

She then painted herself and children, paddled her canoe into the swift current of the rapids and began chanting her death song, in which she recounted her former happy life, with her husband, when she enjoyed his undivided affection, and the wretchedness in which she was now involved by his infidelity. Her friends, alarmed at her imminent peril, ran to the shore and begged her to paddle out of the current before it was too late, while her parents, rending their clothing and tearing their hair, besought her to come to their arms of love; but all in vain. Her wretchedness was complete and must terminate with her existence! She continued her course till her canoe was borne headlong down the roaring cataract, and it and the deserted, heartbroken wife and the beautiful and innocent children, were dashed to pieces on the rocks below. No traces of the canoe or its occupants were found. Her brothers avenged her death by slaying the treacherous husband of the deserted wife.

> They say that still that song is heard
> Above the mighty torrent's roar,
> When trees are by the night-wind stirred
> And darkness broods on stream and shore.

CHAPTER IV.

AUNT JANE.

The Red Song Woman.

Aunt Jane—the Red Song Woman.

Miss Jane Smith Williamson, the subject of this sketch, was one of the famous missionary women in our land in the nineteenth century. She was widely known among both whites and Indians as "Aunt Jane." The Dakotas also called her "Red Song Woman." She was born at Fair Forest, South Carolina, March 8, 1803. Through her father she was a lineal descendant of the Rev. John Newton and Sir Isaac Newton. Her father was a revolutionary soldier.

Her mother was Jane (Smith) Williamson. They believed that negroes had souls and therefore treated the twenty-seven slaves they had inherited like human beings. Her mother was fined in South Carolina, for teaching her slaves to read the Bible. Consequently, in 1804, in her early infancy, her parents emigrated to Adams county, Ohio, in order to be able to free their slaves and teach them to read the Word of God and write legibly.

The story of Aunt Jane's life naturally falls into three divisions.

I—PREPARATION FOR HER GREAT LIFE WORK.

This covered forty years. She grew up in an atmosphere of sincere and deep piety and of devotion to Christian principles. Her early educational advantages were necessarily limited, but she made the most of them. She became very accurate in the use of language, wrote a clear round hand and was very thorough in everything she studied. She was a great reader of good and useful books, possessed an excellent memory and a lively imagination and very early acquired a most interesting style of composition.

From her ancestors she inherited that strong sympathy for the colored race, which was a marked characteristic of her whole life. In her young womanhood, she taught private schools in Adams county, Ohio. The progress made by her pupils was very rapid and her instruction was of a high order. She sought out the children of the poor and taught them without charge. She admitted colored pupils as well as whites. For this cause, many threats of violence were made against her school. But she was such an excellent teacher that her white pupils remained with her; and a guard of volunteer riflemen frequently surrounded her school house. She calmly pursued the even tenor of her way.

AUNT JANE,

Or, The Red Song Woman.

In 1820, when she was only 17 years of age, she and her brother rode on horseback all the way from Manchester, Ohio, to South Carolina and back again, and brought with them two slaves they had inherited. They could have sold them in the South for $300 each, and stood in great need of the money; but instead, they gave to these two poor colored persons the priceless boon of liberty. Miss Williamson's slave was a young woman of her own age, called Jemima. She was married to another slave named Logan. She was the mother of two children. Logan was a daring man, and rendered desperate by the loss of his young wife, he determined to be free and follow her. He fled from South Carolina, and after passing through many adventures of the most thrilling character, he found his wife in Ohio, and lived and died a free man. He was fully determined to die rather than return to slavery. Jemima lived to a great age, surviving her husband, who was killed accidently in the fifties. They left a family highly respected.

During all these years "Aunt Jane" was a very active worker in Sabbath schools, prayer meetings and missionary societies. In her own day schools, she made religious worship and Bible study a prominent feature of the exercises. In 1835, when her brother, Dr. Williamson, went as a missionary to the Dakotas, she strongly desired to accompany him. But her duty required her to remain at home and care for her aged father, who died in 1839, at the age of 77. She did not join her brother, however, until 1843, at the age of forty.

II—HER WORK AMONG THE DAKOTAS.

This covers one-third of a century. The missionary spirit was a part of her life,—born with her,—a heritage of several generations. The blood of the Newtons flowed in her veins. When she arrived in Minnesota, she went to work without delay and with great energy and with untiring industry greatly beyond her strength. She was very familiar with the Bible. She taught hundreds of Indians, perhaps fully one thousand, to read the Word of God, and the greater part of them to write a legible letter. She visited all the sick within her reach, and devoted much of her time to instructing the Dakota women in domestic duties. She conducted prayer meetings and conversed with them in reference to the salvation of their souls. Many of them, saved by the Holy Spirit's benediction upon her self-denying efforts, are now shining like bright gems in her crown of glory on high.

Lac-qui-Parle,—the Lake-that-speaks,—two hundred miles west of St. Paul, was her first missionary home. There she gathered the young Indians together and taught them as opportunity offered. The instruction of the youth—especially the children, of whom she was ever a devoted lover, was her great delight.

It was more than a year before any mail reached her at this remote outpost. She was absent in the Indian village when she heard of the arrival of her first mail. She, in her eagerness to hear from her friends in Ohio, ran like a young woman to her brother's house. She found the mail in the stove-oven. The carrier had brought it through the ice, and it had to be thawed out. That mail contained more than fifty letters for her and the postage on them was over five dollars. In 1846, she removed with her brother to Kaposia, Little Crow's village (now South St. Paul), and in 1852 to Yellow Medicine, thirty-two miles south of Lac-qui-Parle. The privations of the missionaries were very great. White bread was more of a luxury to them then, than rich cake ordinarily is now. Their houses and furnishings were of the rudest kind. Their environments were all of a savage character.

Their trials were many and sore, extreme scarcity of food in mid-winter, savage threats and bitter insults. They were "in journeyings often, in perils of waters, of robbers, by the heathen and in the wilderness." All this she endured contentedly for Christ's sake and the souls of the poor ignorant savages around for the evangelization and salvation of the degraded Dakotas,—lost in sin.

She possessed great tact and was absolutely fearless. In 1857, during the Inkpadoota trouble, the father of a young-Indian, who had been wounded by the soldiers of Sherman's battery, came with his gun to the mission house to kill her brother. Aunt Jane met him with a plate of food for himself and an offer to send some nice dishes to the wounded young man. This was effectual. The savage was tamed. He ate the food and afterwards came with his son to give them thanks. Scarcely was the prison-camp, with nearly four hundred Dakota prisoners, three-fourths of them condemned to be hanged, established at Mankato, when Aunt Jane and her brother came to distribute paper and pencils and some books among them.

When their lives were imperilled, by their savage pursuers, during the terrible massacre, Aunt Jane calmly said; "Well if they kill me, my home is in Heaven." The churches were scattered, the work apparently destroyed, but nothing could discourage Aunt Jane. She had, in the midst of this great tragedy, the satisfactory knowledge that all the Christian Sioux had continued at the risk of their own lives, steadfast in their loyalty, and had been instrumental in saving the lives of many whites. They had, also, influenced for good many of their own race.

III—THE CLOSING YEARS OF HER LIFE.

After that terrible massacre the way never opened for her to resume her residence among the Dakotas; but she was given health and strength for nineteen years more toil for the Master and her beloved Indians. Her home was with her brother, Dr. Williamson, near St. Peter, until his death in 1879, and she remained, in his old home several years after his death. During this period, she accomplished much for the education of the Indians around her and she kept up an extensive and helpful correspondence with native Christian workers. All the time she kept up the work of self-sacrifice for the good of others. In 1881 she met a poor Indian woman, suffering extremely from intense cold. She slipped off her own warm skirt and gave it to the woman. The result was a severe illness, which caused her partial paralysis and total blindness from which she never recovered. In 1888 she handed the writer a $5 gold coin for the work among the freedmen with this remark: "First the freedman; then the Indian." Out of a narrow income she constantly gave generously to the boards of the church and to the poor around her. She spent most of her patrimony in giving and lending to needy ones.

The closing years of her life were spent with her nephew the great Indian missionary the Rev. John P. Williamson D.D. at Greenwood, South Dakota. There at noon of March 24, 1895, the light of eternity dawned upon her and she entered into that sabbatic rest, which remains for the people of God. Such is the story of Aunt Jane, modest and unassuming—a real heroine, who travelled sixteen hundred miles all the way on horseback and spent several months that she might rescue two poor colored persons whom she had never seen or even known.

Without husband or children, alone in the world, she did not repine, but made herself useful, wherever she was, in teaching secular learning and religious truth, and in ministering to the sick and afflicted, the down-trodden and oppressed. She never sought to do any wonderful things,—but whatever her hand found to do, she did it with her might and with an eye to the honor and glory of God. Hers was a very long and most complete Christian life. Should it ever be forgotten? Certainly not, while our Christian religion endures.

"Blessed are the dead which die in the Lord from henceforth; yea, saith the Spirit, that they may rest from their labors and their works do follow them."

—Rev. 14: 13.

CHAPTER V.

ARTEMAS, THE WARRIOR PREACHER.

Artemas—the Warrior-Preacher.

He was one of the fiercest of the Sioux warriors. He fought the Ojibways in his youth; danced the scalp-dance on the present site of Minneapolis, and waged war against the whites in '62. He was converted at Mankato, Minnesota, in the prison-pen, and for thirty-two years, he was pastor of the Pilgrim Congregational church at Santee, Nebraska.

Artemas Ehnamane was born in 1825, at Red Wing, Minnesota, by the mountain that stands sentinel at the head of Lake Pepin. "Walking Along" is the English translation of his jaw-breaking surname. As a lad, he played on the banks of the mighty Mississippi. As a youth, he hunted the red deer in the lovely glades of Minnesota and Wisconsin. He soon grew tall and strong and became a famous hunter. The war-path, also, opened to him in the pursuit of his hereditary foes, the Chippewas. He danced the scalp-dance on the present site of Minneapolis, when it was only a wind-swept prairie.

While in his youth, his tribe ceded their ancestral lands along the Mississippi and removed to the Sioux Reservation on the Minnesota River. But not for long, for the terrible outbreak of 1862, scattered everything and landed all the leading men of that tribe in prison. Artemas was one of them. He was convicted, condemned to death, and pardoned by Abraham Lincoln. While in the prison-pen at Mankato, he came into a new life "that thinketh no evil of his neighbor." The words of the faithful missionaries, Pond and Williamson and Riggs, sank deep into his heart. His whole nature underwent a change. Artemas once explained his conversion thus:

"We had planned that uprising wisely and secretly. We had able leaders. We were well organized and thoroughly armed. The whites were weakened by the Southern war. Everything was in our favor. We had prayed to our gods. But when the conflict came, we were beaten so rapidly and completely, I felt that the white man's God must be greater than all the Indians' gods; and I determined to look Him up, and I found Him, All-Powerful and precious to my soul."

Faithfully he studied his letters and learned his Dakota Bible, which became more precious to him than any record of traditions and shadows handed down from mouth to mouth by his people. He soon became possessed of a great longing to let his tribe know his great secret of the God above. So when the prisoners were restored to their families in the Missouri Valley in Nebraska, Artemas was soon chosen one of the preachers of the reorganized tribe. His first pastorate was that of the Pilgrim Congregational Church at Santee, Nebraska, in 1867. It was also his last, for he was ever so beloved and honored by his people, that they would not consider any proposal for separation.

No such proposition ever met with favor in the Pilgrim Church for Artemas firmly held first place in the affections of the people among whom he labored so earnestly. He served this church for thirty-two years and passed on to take his place among the Shining Ones, on the eve of Easter Sabbath, 1902.

Artemas seldom took a vacation. In fact there is only one on record. In 1872, his church voted a vacation of six weeks. True to his Indian nature, he planned a deer hunt. He turned his footsteps to the wilds of the Running Water (Niobrara River), where his heart grew young and his rifle cracked the death-knell of the deer and antelope. One evening, in the track of the hostile Sioux and Pawnees, he found himself near a camp of the savage Sicaugu. He was weak and alone. They were strong and hostile.

He had tact as well as courage. He invited those savage warriors to a feast. His kettle was brimming, and as the Indians filled their mouths with the savory meat, he filled their ears with the story of the gospel, and gave them their first view of that eternal life, purchased by the blood of Christ.

The deer-hunt became a soul-hunt. The wild Sicaugu grunted their amicable "Hao" as they left his teepee, their mouths filled with venison and their hearts planted with the seeds of eternal truth.

Again he went on a deer-hunt, when he crossed another trail, that of hunters from another hostile tribe. In the camp he found a sick child, the son of Samuel Heart, a Yankton Sioux. But let Heart tell the story himself in his simple way:

"I was many days travel away in the wilderness. My child was very sick. I felt much troubled. A man of God came to my tent. I remember all he said. He told me not to be troubled, but to trust in God, and all would be well. He prayed; he asked God to strengthen the child so I could bring him home. God heard him. My child lived to get home. Once my heart would have been very sad, and I would have done something very wicked. I look forward and trust Jesus."

This is how Rev. Artemas Ehnamane spent his vacations, hunting for wild souls instead of wild deer.

He was a scriptural, personal and powerful preacher.

Faith in a risen Saviour, was the keynote of his ministry. As he said: "Who of all the Saviours of the Indian people has risen from the dead? Not one." "Our fathers told us many things and gave us many customs, but they were not true." "I grew up believing in what my father taught me, but when I knew of Jesus Christ, the Son of God, I believed in Him and put aside all my ways." It was to him in truth, the coming out of darkness into light. "Sins are like wolves," he said. "They abound in the darkness and destroy men. When we enter the way, Jesus watches over us. Be awake and follow Him. All over the world men are beginning to follow Christ. The day is here." "Repent, believe, obey."

He loved to sing:
"Saved, by grace, alone;
That is all my plea;
Jesus died for all mankind;
Jesus died for me."

The twenty grand-children of the old Sioux—all of school age—are diligently prosecuting their studies in order to be prepared to meet the changed conditions which civilization has made possible for the Indians. One of his grand-sons is a physician now, in a fair practice among his own people.

This man President Lincoln wisely pardoned, knowing full well what a great influence for good such a man could wield over his turbulent people. And the President was not disappointed. One of his sons has been a missionary among the Swift Bear tribe at the Rose Bud Agency for twenty years; another son has been a missionary at Standing Rock, on the Grand River, and is now pastor of an Indian congregation on Basile Creek, Nebraska, and is also an important leader of his tribe. The Rev. Francis Frazier, one of his sons, was installed September 10, 1902, as his father's successor in the pastorate of Pilgrim church at Santee.

His married daughter is also very earnest in the woman's work in the church. Seventy-seven years of age at his death, Rev. Artemas Ehnamane had filled to overflowing with good deeds to offset the first half, when he fought against the encroachments of the whites and the advance of civilization with as much zeal as later he evinced in his religious and beneficent life. Abraham Lincoln pardoned Ehnamane and the old warrior never forgot it. But it was another pardon he prized more highly than that. It was this pardon he preached and died believing.

CHAPTER VI.

TWO FAMOUS MISSIONS.

Lake Harriet and Prairieville.

Two Famous Missions—Lake Harriet and Prairieville.

LAKE HARRIET.

In the spring of 1835, the Rev. Jedediah Dwight Stevens, of the Presbyterian Church, arrived at Fort Snelling under the auspices of the American Board of Missions. He established a station on the northwestern shore of Lake Harriet. It was a most beautiful spot, west of the Indian village, presided over by that friendly and influential chieftain Cloudman or Man-of-the-sky. He erected two buildings—the mission-home, first residence for white settlers, and the school house—the first building erected exclusively for school purposes within the present boundaries of the State of Minnesota.

Within a few rods of the Pavilion, where on the Sabbath, multitudes gather for recreation, and desecration of God's holy day, is the site, where, in 1835, the first systematic effort was made to educate and Christianize Dakota Indians. It is near the present junction of Forty-second Street, and Queen Avenue (Linden Hills).

In July, Mr. Stevens, and his interesting family, took possession of the mission house. With the co-operation of the Pond brothers, this mission was prosecuted with a fair measure of success till the removal of the Indians farther west, in 1839, when it was abandoned, and the connection of Mr. Stevens with the work of the Dakota mission ceased.

Here on the evening of November 22, 1838, a romantic wedding was solemnized by Rev. J. D. Stevens. The groom was Samuel Pond of the Dakota mission. The groomsman was Henry H. Sibley, destined in after years to be Minnesota's first delegate to Congress, her first state executive, and in the trying times of '62, the victorious General Sibley. The bride was Miss Cordelia Eggleston; the bridesmaid, Miss Cornelia Stevens; both amiable, lovely and remarkably handsome.

It was a brilliant, starry evening, one of Minnesota's brightest and most invigorating. The sleighing was fine, and among the guests, were many officers, from Fort Snelling, with their wives. Dr. Emerson and wife, the owners of Dred Scott, the subject of Judge Taney's infamous decision, were present. The doctor was, then, post-surgeon at the fort, and the slave Dred, was his body-servant. The tall bridegroom and groomsman, in the vigor and strength of their young manhood; the bride and bridesmaid, just emerging from girlhood, with all their dazzling beauty, the officers in the brilliant uniforms, and their wives, in their gay attire, must have formed an attractive picture in the long ago. After the wedding festivities, the guests from the fort were imprisoned at the mission for the night, by a blizzard, which swept over the icy face of Lake Harriet.

In the previous November, at Lac-qui-Parle, the younger brother was united in marriage to Miss Sarah Poage, by the Rev. Stephen R. Riggs. It was a unique gathering. The guests were all the dark-faced dwellers of the Indian village, making a novel group of whites, half-breeds and savage Indians. Many of the latter were poor, maimed, halt and blind, who thoroughly enjoyed the feast of potatoes, turnips, and bacon so generously provided by the happy bridegroom.

PRAIRIEVILLE.

In 1846, Shakpe or Little Six, extended an urgent invitation to Samuel Pond to establish a mission at Tintonwan—"the village on the prairies"—for the benefit of his people. He was chief of one of the most turbulent bands of Indians in the valley of the Minnesota. He was a man of marked ability and one of the ablest and most effective orators in the whole Dakota nation. Yet withal, Shakpe was a petty thief, had a "forked tongue," a violent temper, was excitable, and vindictive in his revenge. These characteristics led him to the scaffold. He was hanged at Fort Snelling, in 1863 for participation in the bloody massacre of '62. He and his followers were so noted for their deception and treachery, that Mr. Pond doubted their sincerity and the wisdom of accepting their invitation. But after weeks of prayerful deliberation, he accepted and began preparations for a permanent establishment at that point. He erected a commodious and substantial residence into which he removed, with his household, in November 1847.

This station, which Mr. Pond called Prairieville, was fourteen miles southeast of Oak Grove mission, on the present site of Shakopee. The mission home was pleasantly located on gently rising ground, half a mile south of the Minnesota River. It was surrounded by the teepees of six hundred noisy savages. Here, for several years they toiled unceasingly for the welfare of the wild men, by whom they were surrounded.

In 1851, Mr. and Mrs. Pond were compelled, by her rapidly failing health, to spend a year in the east. She never returned. She died February 6, 1852, at Washington, Connecticut. Thus after fourteen years of arduous missionary toil, Cordelia Eggleston Pond, the beautiful bride of the Lake Harriet mission house, was called from service to reward at the early age of thirty-six.

Mr. Pond returned to Prairieville and toiled on for the Indians until their removal by the government, in 1853. He himself, remained and continued his labors for the benefit of the white community of Shakopee, which had grown up around him. In 1853, a white Presbyterian church was organized and, in 1856, a comfortable church edifice was erected, wholly at the expense of the pastor and his people. The congregation still exists and the mission house still stands as monuments of the wisdom, faith and fortitude of the heroic builder. After thirteen years of faithful service, he laid the heavy burdens down for younger hands, but for a quarter of a century longer he remained in his old home.

During these last years, his chief delight was in his books, which lost none of their power to interest him in advancing age; especially was this true of the Book of books. He was never idle. The active energy, which distinguished his youth, no less marked his advancing years. His mind was as clear, his judgment as sound, and his mental vision as keen at eighty-three, as they were at thirty-three. His was a long and happy old age. He lingered in the house his own hands had builded, content to go or stay, till he was transferred, December twelfth, 1891, to the house not made with hands, eternal in the heavens.

CHAPTER VII.

THE PRINCE OF INDIAN PREACHERS.

The Prince of Indian Preachers.

Without disparagement to any of his brethren in the ministry, this title can be properly applied to the Rev. John Baptiste Renville, of Iyakaptapte, (Ascension) South Dakota, who recently passed on to join the shining ranks of the saved Sioux in glory.

Timid as a little child, yet bold as a lion, when aroused; shy of conversation in private, yet eloquent in the pulpit and in the council-chamber; yielding yet firm as a rock, when duty demanded it; a loving husband, a kind father, a loyal citizen, a faithful presbyter—a pungent preacher of the gospel, a soul-winner—a courteous, cultured Christian gentleman; such a man was this Indian son of a Sioux mother, herself the first fullblood Sioux convert to the Christian faith.

He was the youngest son of Joseph Renville, a mixed blood Sioux and French, who was a captain in the British army in the War of 1812 and the most famous Sioux Indian in his day. After the war, he became a trader and established his headquarters at Lac-qui-Parle, where he induced Dr. Thomas S. Williamson to locate his first mission station in 1835.

John Baptiste was one of the first Indian children baptized by Dr. Williamson and he enjoyed the benefits of the first school among the Sioux. He was rather delicate, which hindered his being sent east to school as much as he otherwise would have been. However, he spent several years in excellent white schools, and he acquired a fair knowledge of the elementary branches of the English language. The last year he spent at Knox College, Galesburgh, Illinois, where he wooed and won Miss Mary Butler, an educated Christian white woman, whom he married and who became his great helper in his educational and evangelistic work.

He was the first Sioux Indian to enter the ministry. In the spring of 1865, he was licensed to preach, by the presbytery of Dakota, at Mankato, Minnesota, and ordained in the following autumn. When he entered the ministry, the Sioux Indians we're in a very unsettled state, and his labors were very much scattered; now with the Indian scouts on some campaign; again with a few families of Indians gathered about some military post, and anon with a little class of Indians, who were trying to settle down to civilized life.

**JOHN B. RENVILLE[1] JOHN P. WILLIAMSON, D.D. DANIEL RENVILLE
JOHN EASTMAN CHARLES R. CRAWFORD**

All Indian Ministers Except Dr. Williamson

THE REV. THOMAS S. WILLIAMSON, M.D.,

Forty-five years a Missionary to the Sioux.

____

[1] Died Dec. 19, 1904

In 1870, he became the pastor of Iyakaptapte, (Ascension) a little church in what subsequently became the Sisseton reservation. Both physically and in mental and spiritual qualities, he was best adapted to a settled pastorate. His quiet and unobtrusive character required long intercourse to be appreciated. However, in the pulpit, his earnestness and apt presentation of the truth ever commanded the attention even of strangers. Under his ministry, the church increased to one hundred and forty members. More than half a dozen of them became ministers and Ascension was generally the leading church in every good work among the Dakota Indians. No one among the Christian Sioux was more widely known and loved than Mr. Renville. In the councils of the church, though there were seventeen other ministers in the presbytery before his death, he was ever given the first place both for counsel and honor. He twice represented his presbytery in the general Assembly, and he was ever faithful in his attendance at Synod and Presbytery and active in the discharge of the duties devolving upon him.

Mary Butler, the white wife of his youth, died several years ago. Their daughter Ella, a fine Christian young lady passed away at twenty years of age. She was active in organizing Bands of Hope among the children of the tribe. She sleeps, with her parents on the brow of Iyakaptapte overlooking the church to which all their lives were devoted. Josephine, the Indian wife of his old age, survives him and remains in the white farm house on the prairie in which John Baptiste Renville spent so many years of his long, happy useful life. He died December 19, 1904, in the seventy-third year of his age.

CHAPTER VIII.
AN INDIAN PATRIARCH.

An Indian Patriarch.

Chief Cloudman or Man-of-the-sky, was one of the strongest characters among the natives on the headwaters of the Mississippi in the earlier half of the nineteenth century. He was one of the leading chiefs of the Santee band of Sioux Indians. He was born about 1780. He was brave in battle, wise in council, and possessed many other noble qualities, which caused him to rise far above his fellow chieftains. He possessed a large fund of common sense. Years prior to the advent of the white man in this region, he regarded hunting and fishing as a too precarious means to a livelihood, and attempted to teach his people agriculture and succeeded to a limited extent.

REV. JOHN EASTMAN.

It was a strange circumstance that prompted the chief to this wise action. On a hunting tour in the Red River country, with a part of his band, they were overtaken by a drifting storm and remained, for several days, under the snow, without any food whatsoever. While buried in those drifts, he resolved to rely, in part, upon agriculture, for subsistence, if he escaped alive, and he carried out his resolution, after the immediate peril was passed. His band cultivated small fields of quickly maturing corn, which had been introduced by their chief in the early 30's. He was respected and loved by his people and quite well obeyed.

Before the coming of the missionaries he taught and enforced, by his example, this principle, namely, that it as wrong to kill non-combatants, or to kill under any circumstances in time of peace. He favored peace rather than war. He was twenty-five years of age, and had six notches on the handle of his tomahawk, indicating that he had slain half a dozen of his Ojibway foes before he adopted this human policy.

His own band lived on the shores of Lakes Calhoun and Harriet, within the present limits of Minneapolis. On the present site of lovely Lakewood—Minneapolis' most fashionable cemetery—was his village of several hundred savages, and also an Indian burial place. This village was the front guard against the war parties of the Ojibways—feudal enemies of the Sioux—but finally as their young men were killed off in battle, they were compelled to remove and join their people on the banks of the Minnesota and farther West. He located his greatly reduced band at Bloomington, directly west of his original village. This removal occurred prior to 1838.

He was never hostile to the approach of civilization, or blind to the blessings it might confer on his people.

He was one of the first of his tribe to accept the white man's ways and to urge his band to follow his example. This fact is confirmed by the great progress his descendants have made.

He was the first Sioux Indian of any note to welcome those first pioneer missionaries, the Pond brothers. As early as 1834 he encouraged them to erect their home and inaugurate their work in his village. In all the treaties formed between the government and the Sioux, he was ever the ready and able advocate of the white man's cause. He threw all the weight of his powerful influence in favor of cession to the United States government of the military reservation on which Fort Snelling now stands. He died at Fort Snelling in 1863, and was buried on the banks of the Minnesota in view of the fort.

He was the father of seven children, all of whom are dead, except his son David Weston, his successor in the chieftainship, who still lives at Flandreau, South Dakota, at the age of seventy-eight years. He was for many years a catechist of the Episcopal Church. His two daughters were called Hushes-the-Night and Stands-like-a-Spirit. They were once the belles of Lake Harriet, to whom the officers and fur traders paid homage. Hushes-the-Night married a white man named Lamont and became the mother of a child called Jane. She had one sister, who died childless, in St. Paul, in 1901. Jane Lamont married Star Titus, a nephew of the

Pond brothers. They became the parents of three sons and two daughters. Two of these sons are bankers and rank among the best business men of North Dakota. They are recognized as leaders among the whites. The other son is a farmer near Tracy, Minnesota. Stands-Like-a-Spirit was the mother of one daughter, Mary Nancy Eastman, whose father, Captain Seth Eastman, was stationed at Fort Snelling—1830-36. Mary Nancy married Many Lightnings, a fullblood, one of the leaders of the Wahpeton-Sioux. They became the parents of four sons and one daughter. After Many Lightnings became a Christian, he took his wife's name, Eastman, instead of his own, and gave all his children English names. John the eldest, and Charles Alexander, the youngest son, have made this branch of the Cloudman family widely and favorably known.

John Eastman, at twenty-six years of age, became a Presbyterian minister, and for more than a quarter of a century has been the successful pastor of the First Presbyterian church of Flandreau, South Dakota. He was for many years a trusty Indian agent at that place. He is a strong factor in Indian policy and politics. He has had a scanty English education in books, but he has secured an excellent training, chiefly by mingling with cultured white people.

His proud statement once was; "every adult member of the Flandreau band is a professing Christian, and every child of school age is in school." During the "Ghost Dance War," in 1890, his band remained quietly at home, busy about their affairs. In the spring of 1891, they divided $40,000 among themselves.

Charles Alexander Eastman was born in 1858, in Minnesota, the ancestral home of the Sioux, and passed the first fifteen years of his life in the heart of the wilds of British America, enjoying to the full, the free, nomadic existence of his race. During all this time, he lived in a teepee of buffalo skins, subsisted upon wild rice and the fruits of the chase, never entered a house nor heard the English language spoken, and was taught to distrust and hate the white man.

The second period (third) of his life was spent in school and college, where after a short apprenticeship in a mission school, he stood shoulder to shoulder, with our own youth, at Beloit, Knox, Dartmouth and the Boston university. He is an alumnus of Dartmouth of '87 and of Boston University, department of medicine, of '90.

During the last fifteen years, he has been a man of varied interests and occupations, a physician, missionary, writer and speaker of wide experience and, for the greater part of the time, has held an appointment under the government.

At his birth he was called "Hakadah" or "The Pitiful Last," as his mother died shortly after his birth. He bore this sad name till years afterwards he was called Ohiyesa, "The Winner," to commemorate a great victory of La Crosse, the Indian's favorite game, won by his band, "The Leaf Dwellers," over their foes, the Ojibways. When he received this new name, the leading medicine man thus exhorted him: "Be brave, be patient and thou shalt always win. Thy name is "Ohiyesa the Winner."" The spirit of his benediction seems to follow and rest upon him in his life-service.

His grandmother was "Stands-Like-a-Spirit," the second daughter of the old chief Cloudman. His full-blooded Sioux father was a remarkable man in many ways and his mother, a half-blood woman, was the daughter of a well-known army officer. She was the most beautiful woman of the "Leaf Dwellers" band. By reason of her great beauty, she was called "Demi-Goddess of the Sioux." Save for her luxuriant, black hair, and her deep black eyes, she had every characteristic of Caucasian descent. The motherless lad was reared by his grandmother and an uncle in the wilds of Manitoba, where he learned thoroughly, the best of the ancient folk lore, religion and woodcraft of his people. Thirty years of civilization have not dimmed his joy in the life of the wilderness nor caused him to forget his love and sympathy for the primitive people and the animal friends, who were the intimates of his boyhood.

DR. CHARLES A. EASTMAN,

Famous Sioux Author, Orator and Physician.

He is very popular as a writer for the leading magazines. "His Recollections of Wild Life" in St. Nicholas, and his stories of "Wild Animals" in Harper, have entertained thousands of juvenile as well as adult readers. His first book, "Indian boyhood," which appeared in 1902, has passed through several editions, and met with hearty appreciation. "Red Hunters and the Animal People," published in 1904, bids fair to be, at least, equally popular.

During the last two years, he has lectured in many towns from Maine to California and he is welcomed everywhere. His specialty is the customs, laws, religion, etc., of the Sioux. Witty, fluent, intellectual, trained in both methods of education, he is eminently fitted to explain, in an inimitable and attractive manner, the customs, beliefs and superstitions of the Indian. He describes not only the life and training of the boy, but the real Indian as no white man could possibly do. He brings out strongly the red man's wit, music, poetry and eloquence. He also explains graphically from facts gained from his own people, the great mystery of the battle of the Little Big Horn in which the gallant Custer and brave men went to their bloody death.

He was married in 1891 at New York City, to Miss Elaine Goodale, a finely cultured young lady from Massachusetts, herself a poetess and prose writer of more than ordinary ability.

They have lived very happily together ever since and are the parents of five lovely children. They have lived in Washington and St. Paul and are now residents of Amherst, Massachusetts. Whether in his physician's office, in his study, on the lecture platform, in the press or in his own home, Dr. Charles Alexander Eastman is a most attractive personality.

CHAPTER IX.

JOHN.

The Beloved of the Sioux Nation.

John—the Beloved of the Sioux Nation.

Rev. John P. Williamson, D.D., of Greenwood, South Dakota, was born in the month of October, 1835, in one of Joseph Renville's log cabins, with dirt roof and no floor; and was the first white child born in Minnesota, outside of the soldier's families at Fort Snelling. His father, the Rev. Thomas S. Williamson. M.D., was the first ordained missionary appointed to labor among the Sioux Indians. He came out to the new Northwest on an exploring expedition in 1834, visiting the Indian camps at Wabawsha, Red Wing, Kaposia, and others.

He returned in the spring of 1835, with his family and others who were appointed.

After the arrival of this missionary party, Dr. Williamson and his colleagues, lived and labored continuously among the Indians the remainder of their lives. Their work for the Master has not suffered any interruption, but is still carried on successfully and vigorously by their successors.

John P. Williamson grew up in the midst of the Indians. He mastered the Sioux language in early boyhood. As a lad, he had the present sites of Minneapolis and St. Paul for his playgrounds and little Indian lads for his playmates. Among these, was Little Crow, who afterwards became infamous in his savage warfare, against the defenseless settlers in western Minnesota, in 1862.

He was early dedicated to the work of the gospel ministry. In his young manhood he was sent to Ohio, for his education. In 1857, he graduated at Marietta College, and in 1860, at Lane Seminary, Cincinnati. In 1859 he was licensed by Dakota (Indian) Presbytery, and ordained, by the same body, in 1861. The degree of D.D. was conferred upon him by Yankton, (S.D.) college in 1890. He recognized no call to preach the gospel save to the Sioux Indians, and for forty-six years, he has given his whole life zealously to this great work. He has thrown his whole life unreservedly into it. And he has accomplished great things for the Master and the tribe to which he has ministered.

In 1860 he established a mission and organized a Presbyterian church of twelve members at Red Wood Agency on the Minnesota. These were both destroyed in the outbreak two years later. He spent the winter of 1862-3, in evangelistic work, among the Sioux, in the prison-camp at Fort Snelling, where 1,500 were gathered under military guard. An intense religious interest sprung up amongst them and continued for months. Young Dr. Williamson so ministered unto them, that the whole camp was reached and roused, and the major part of the adults were led to Christ. Many, including scores of the children of the believers, were baptized. A Presbyterian congregation of more than one hundred communicants was organized. This church was afterwards united with the church of the Prison-pen, at Crow Creek, Nebraska.

In 1883, he was appointed superintendent of Presbyterian missions among the Sioux Indians. He has ever abounded in self-sacrificing and successful labors among this tribe. He has organized Nineteen (19) congregations and erected twenty-three (23) church edifices. In twenty-three years he has traveled two hundred thousand miles in the prosecution of these arduous labors. The number of converts cannot be reckoned up.

In 1866, he was married to Miss Sarah A. Vannice. To them there have been born four sons and three daughters, who are still living. In 1869 he established the Yankton mission, which has ever since been a great center, moral and spiritual, to a vast region. At the same time he established his home at Greenwood, South Dakota, and from that, as his mission headquarters, he has gone to and from in his great missionary tours throughout the Dakota land.

He has, also, abounded in literary labors. For sixteen years he was the chief editor of "Iapi Oayi," an Indian weekly. In 1864, he published "Powa Wow-spi," an Indian Spelling Book, and in 1865, a collection of Dakota Hymns. His greatest literary work, however, was an edition of the "Dakota Dictionary," in 1871, and other later editions.

He has won the affections of the whole Sioux nation. They bow willingly to his decisions, and follow gladly his counsels. To them, he is a much greater man than President Roosevelt. While he has passed the limit of his three-score years and ten—forty-six of them in frontier service—his bow still abides in strength, and he still abounds in manifold labors. He is still bringing forth rich fruitage in his old age.

Every white dweller among the Indians is known by some special cognomen. His is simply "John." And when it is pronounced, by a Sioux Indian as a member of the tribe always does it so lovingly, all who hear it know he refers to "John, the Beloved of the Sioux Nation."

CHAPTER X.

THE MARTYRS OF OLD ST. JOE.

The Martyrs of Old St. Joe.

One of the most touching tragedies recorded in the annals of the new North-west, was enacted in the sixth decade of the nineteenth century, on the borders of Prince Rupert's Land and the Louisiana purchase (now Manitoba and North Dakota). It is a picturesque spot, where the Pembina river cuts the international boundary line in its course to the southeast to join the Red River of the North in its course to Hudson's bay.

Sixty years ago, in this place, encircled by the wood-crowned mountain and the forest-lined river and prairies, rich as the gardens of the gods, there stood a village and trading post of considerable importance, named after the patron saint of the Roman Catholic church, in its midst—St. Joseph—commonly called St. Joe. It was a busy, bustling town, with a mixed population of 1,500. Most of these dwelt in tents of skin. There were, also, two or three large trading posts and thirty hous-es, built of large, hewn timbers mudded smoothly within and without and roofed with shingles. Some of these were neat and pretty; one had window-shutters. It was the center of an extensive fur trade with the Indian tribes of the Missouri river. Many thousands of buffalo and other skins were shipped annually to St. Paul in carts. Sometimes a train of four hundred of these wooden carts started together for St. Paul, a distance of four hundred miles.

But old things have passed away. The village of old St. Joe is now marked only by some cellar excavations. It possesses, however, a sad interest as the scene of the martyrdom of Protestant missionaries on this once wild frontier, then so far removed from the abodes of civilization.

James Tanner was a converted half-breed, who with his wife labored, in 1849, as a missionary at Lake Winnibogosh, Minnesota. His father had been stolen, when a lad, from his Kentucky home, by the Indians. Near the close of 1849 he visited a brother in the Pembina region. He became so deeply interested in the ig-norant condition of the people there, that he made a tour of the East in their behalf. He visited New York, Washington and other cities, and awakened considerable interest in behalf of the natives of this region. While east he became a member of the Baptist Church. He returned to St. Joe, in 1852, accompanied by a young man named Benjamin Terry, of St. Paul, to open a mission among the Pembina Chip-pewas and half breeds under the auspices of the Baptist Missionary Society. Terry was very slight and youthful in appearance, quiet and retiring in disposition and was long spoken of, by the half-breeds, as "Tanner's Boy." They visited the Red River (Selkirk) settlement (now Winnipeg). While there, Terry wooed and won one of the daughters of the Selkirk settlers, a dark-eyed handsome Scotch lass, to whom he expected to be married in a few months. But, alas, ere the close of summer, he was waylaid, by a savage Sioux, shot full of arrows, his arm broken and his entire scalp carried away. Mr. Tanner secured permission to bury him in the Roman Catholic Cemetery in the corner reserved for suicides, heretics and unbaptized infants. Thus ended in blood, the first effort to establish a Protestant mission in the Pembina country.

June 1, 1853, a band of Presbyterian missionaries arrived at St. Joe. It was composed of the Reverends Alonzo Barnard and David Brainard Spencer, their wives and children. They came in canoes and in carts from Red and Cass lakes, Minnesota, where for ten years, they had labored as missionaries among the Chippewas. They removed to St. Joe, at the earnest request of Governor Alexander Ramsey, of Minnesota, and others familiar with their labors and the needs of the Pembina natives. Mrs. Barnard's health soon gave way. Her husband removed her to the Selkirk settlement, one hundred miles to the north, for medical aid. Her health continued to fail so rapidly that by her strong desire they attempted to return to St. Joe. The first night they encamped in a little tent on the bleak northern plain in the midst of a fierce windstorm. The chilling winds penetrated the folds of the tent. All night long the poor sufferer lay in her husband's arms, moaning constantly: "Hold me close; oh, hold me close." They were compelled to return to the settlement, where after a few days more of intense suffering, she died, Oct. 22, 1853, of quick consumption, caused by ten years exposure and suffering for the welfare of the Indians.

Mrs. Barnard was first interred at the Selkirk settlement, in Prince Rupert's Land (now Manitoba). In the absence of other clergymen, Mr. Barnard was compelled to officiate at his wife's funeral himself. In obedience to her dying request, Mrs. Barnard's remains were removed to St. Joe and re-interred in the yard of the humble mission cabin, Dec. 3, 1853.

In 1854, Mr. Barnard visited Ohio to provide a home for his children. On his return, at Belle Prairie, Minnesota, midway between St. Paul and St. Joe, he met Mr. Spencer and his three motherless children, journeying four hundred miles by ox-cart to St. Paul. There in the rude hovel in which they spent the night, Mr. Barnard baptized Mr. Spencer's infant son, now an honored minister of the Congregational church in Wisconsin. On his arrival at St. Joe Mr. Barnard found another mound close by the grave of his beloved wife.

The story of this third grave is, also, written in blood. It was Aug. 30, 1854. The hostile Sioux were infesting the Pembina region. Only the previous month, had Mrs. Spencer written to a far distant friend in India: "Last December the Lord gave us a little son, whose smiling face cheers many a lonely hour." On this fatal night, she arose to care for this darling boy. A noise at the window attracted her attention. She withdrew the curtain to ascertain the cause. Three Indians stood there with loaded rifles and fired. Three bullets struck her, two in her throat and one in her breast. She neither cried out nor spoke, but reeling to her bed, with her babe in her arms, knelt down, where she was soon discovered by her husband, when he returned from barricading the door. She suffered intensely for several hours and then died. And till daybreak Mr. Spencer sat in a horrid dream, holding his dead wife in his arms. The baby lay in the rude cradle near by, bathed in his mother's blood. The two elder children stood by terrified and weeping. Such was the distressing scene which the neighbors beheld in the morning, when they came with their proffers of sympathy and help. The friendly half-breeds came in, cared for the poor children and prepared the dead mother for burial. A half-breed dug the grave and nailed a rude box together for a coffin. Then with a bleeding heart, the sore bereaved man consigned to the bosom of the friendly earth the remains of his murdered wife.

Within the past thirty years civilization has rapidly taken possession of this lovely region. Christian homes and Christian churches cover these rich prairies. The prosperous and rapidly growing village of Walhalla (Paradise) nestles in the bosom of this lovely vale and occupies contentedly the former site of Old St. Joe.

June 21, 1888, one of the most interesting events in the history of North Dakota occurred at the Presbyterian cemetery, which crowns the brow of the mountain, overlooking Walhalla. It was the unveiling of the monument erected by the Woman's Synodical Missionary Society of North Dakota, which they had previously erected to the memory of Sarah Philena Barnard and Cornelia Spencer, two of the three "Martyrs of St. Joe." The monument is a beautiful and appropriate one of white marble. The broken pieces of old stone formerly placed on Mrs. Barnard's grave, long scattered and lost, were discovered, cemented together and placed upon her new grave. The Rev. Alonzo Barnard, seventy-one years of age, accompanied by his daughter, was present. Standing upon the graves of the martyrs, with tremulous voice and moistened eyes, he gave to the assembled multitude a history of their early missionary toil in the abodes of savagery. It was a thrilling story, the interest intensified by the surroundings. The half-breed women who prepared Mrs. Spencer's body for the burial and who washed and dressed the little babe after his baptism in his mother's blood, were present. The same half-breed who dug Mrs. Spencer's grave in 1854 dug the new grave in 1888. Several pioneers familiar with the facts of the tragedy at the time of its occurrence were also present.

"The Martyr's Plot," the last resting place of these devoted servants of our Lord Jesus Christ, is a beautiful spot, on the hillside, in the Presbyterian Cemetery at Walhalla. It is enclosed by a neat fence, and each of these three martyr's graves is marked by a white stone, with an appropriate inscription.

The Rev. Alonzo Barnard retired to Michigan, where he gave five years of missionary toil to the Chippewas at Omene and many other years of helpful service to the white settlers at other points in that state. In 1883 he retired from the work of the active ministry and spent the remainder of his days with his children.

He died April 14, 1905, at Pomona, Michigan, at the home of his son, Dr. James Barnard, in the eighty-eighth year of his age. There is a large and flourishing Episcopal Indian church at Leech Lake, Minnesota, the scene of Mr. Barnard's labors from 1843-52.

The rector is the Rev. Charles T. Wright, a full-blood Chippewa. He is the eldest son of that famous chieftain, Gray Cloud and is now himself, chief of all the Chippewas. "Thus one soweth and another reapeth."

Lector House believes that a society develops through a two-fold approach of continuous learning and adaptation, which is derived from the study of classic literary works spread across the historic timeline of literature records. Therefore, we aim at reviving, repairing and redeveloping all those inaccessible or damaged but historically as well as culturally important literature across subjects so that the future generations may have an opportunity to study and learn from past works to embark upon a journey of creating a better future.

This book is a result of an effort made by Lector House towards making a contribution to the preservation and repair of original ancient works which might hold historical significance to the approach of continuous learning across subjects.

HAPPY READING & LEARNING!

LECTOR HOUSE LLP
E-MAIL: lectorpublishing@gmail.com